"From page one, Lent dives in with pr̲ meetings. This guide can change your m̲ collaborative decision-making engines. W ᴗ w.

Jodi Detjen, Professor of Management, Suffolk University
co-author, **The Orange Line: A Woman's Guide to Integrating Career, Life and Family** (2013)

"Ever since seeing John Cleese's *"Meetings, Bloody Meetings"* many years ago, I have been looking for ways to improve meetings, either actively or as 'victim.' But most advice you get is around what you should not do, little on what you should do, almost nothing on how you should do it, and with respect to the 'why' I always pulled a blank. Until now! Dr. Lent's *Leading Great Meetings* is addressing all of these questions, concisely and pragmatically. He provides clear advice on how meetings can be structured, run, and made more effective. He includes the rationale for selecting specific tools that actually work when you follow the succinct instructions provided. Finally the remedy for years of pain!"

Dr. Hendrik Seliger, Vice President, Supply Chain Management at Carl Zeiss SMT

"Rick has given us the greatest gift one can as an expert of his craft. *Leading Great Meetings* is the source for masterfully running meetings in the 21st century. This is a core element to creating Authentic Organizations!"

Nick Craig, President, Authentic Leadership Institute
co-author, **Finding Your True North** (2008)

"Meetings are the engine of collaborative work. Organizing effective meetings is not always easy. It takes more than good intentions. It takes planning and effective methods. *Leading Great Meetings* provides a straightforward summary of effective designs for planning and conducting effective meetings, and generating the results we all desire. The tool chest provides an easy, clear reference to all 32 tools. The 12 choices of meeting design are useful for meetings of all types—business, community associations, church groups, even a government bureaucracy like I work in!"

Jim Schlosser, MD, MBA Director, VISN Improvement Resource Office, VA New England Healthcare System

"Finally, someone has decoded the 'secret sauce' to creating good meetings. Rick Lent's *Leading Great Meetings* is an extremely practical guide to designing and running productive, worthwhile meetings that produce results. There is enough theory in the book to explain why things work; however, Dr. Lent has also provided a highly-structured, easy-to-follow approach to designing and running successful meetings. The book's advice and tools range from helping to determine what the meeting's goals are and who should attend right down to a step-by-step, how-to guide for making meetings actually work. These tools and ideas are based on Dr. Lent's many years of leading productive meetings around the world for a wide range of clients. In this book, he has distilled his experience into an easy-to-understand guide. If you run meetings, you should get a copy of this book. You and everyone who attends your meetings will benefit!"

Joseph J. Durzo, Ph.D., Executive Vice President, Énergie Lighting

"In my early years at NASA and then Polaroid, I thought that meetings just flowed naturally like water. I wondered why they took so long and failed to deliver results. Then I learned about up-front framing and saw meetings improve. The tools described in this book will take meeting effectiveness to yet a higher level."

Roy Miller, Ph.D., Vice President of Business Development, 3Derm Systems

"With this book as your guide, you will see meetings in new ways, see options you never knew you had, and realize potential in people you never knew was there. Highly recommended."

Jay Vogt, Peoplesworth
author, **Recharge Your Team** (2009)

"*Leading Great Meetings* is an invaluable resource for anyone planning, designing, and leading a meeting. I don't know anyone who knows more about what it takes to run a successful meeting than Rick Lent, and he put everything he knows into a well-written book and toolkit. This book is the meeting equivalent of Strunk & White's *Elements of Style;* it is a timeless resource you will keep coming back to reference."

Breck Arnzen, President, ArnzenGroup LLC

Leading Great Meetings:

How to Structure Yours for Success

**Tools for Achieving Results with
Face-to-Face and Virtual Meetings**

Richard M. Lent, Ph.D.

Published by Meeting for Results
ISBN 13: 978-0692446003

Library of Congress Control Number: 2015907882

Meeting for Results, Stow, MA
www.meetingforresults.com

Book and cover design: Betsy Stepp, Fiddlehead Graphic Design
Editor: Susan Rardin
Author photo: Susan Avery
House structure photo: Rick Lent

To Sharon

who has supported me in so many ways
as my partner on this journey.

Contents

PART VII: Why You Can Trust These Recommendations   **121**

Part VIII: The Tool Chest   **127**

Introduction

It Began with Two Insights

Can leaders run more productive meetings without special facilitation skills? Two key insights helped me answer this question with a resounding "yes." The first insight came while I was facilitating various large group meetings. In these situations I would be helping 50, 100, or more participants reach decisions and plan actions in a limited amount of time. I had learned methods, (e.g., Future Search), that enabled me to lead these sessions with reliably great results. Such methods do not rely on behavior changes or meeting norms. Instead, they utilized meeting structure to help people talk together. Specific structures made more productive behavior natural. My insight came when I realized that *some techniques of these large group methods could improve smaller, "regular" meetings led by someone without specific facilitation training.* To date, however, only a small group of specialized facilitators knew anything about them.

A second insight came after I helped the chair of a town committee design and run a series of community meetings. Her challenge was to find a way to engage local residents in choosing among options to a difficult town planning decision. The usual approach to committee meetings using a formal room set-up and discussion process had led to difficult exchanges with town members. I recommended that we move the sessions to more flexible spaces and use a structure that supported dialogue and constructive feedback. The subsequent sessions went well and the town reached a widely supported decision. Later, a town leader asked me why these meetings were so successful. I asked him if he had noticed any significant differences in how they were conducted. He said he was surprised that there was no head table and that

See chapter 15 for the full story of this meeting and its structure.

there were clusters of chairs with opportunities to have small group discussions with committee members. He concluded that we made the best use we could out of a non-traditional meeting space but hadn't thought much more about it. When I explained that none of this was accidental, that the structure of these meetings was intentional, he paused and said that he could see this now—but he hadn't seen it then. This exchange gave me my second insight. I realized that *people may not recognize or even see the structures that shape meeting behaviors and outcomes.* To use structure to create better meetings, leaders must first be more aware of the structural choices they have for the meetings they run.

Seeing Structure and Its Influence

Meeting "structure" includes physical, temporal, and procedural variables that influence how people talk together. People act as they do in a given structure because that's what makes sense to them to do—sometimes without even thinking about it. We don't recognize the significance of group size, agenda design, who sits where, or who speaks, and so don't "see" structure's impact. Instead, we focus our attention on the content and interpersonal dynamics of the discussion.

Meeting structure works much like this house's structure. Underlying structure determines how the finished house will function even while beams and masonry remain unseen.

A familiar example of structure's influence

One example of "unseen" structure involves the impact of group size on engagement. Many leaders become frustrated when participants do not remain fully engaged in some discussion. But size matters. Meetings with more than eight participants have a different structure and different challenges than smaller groups. In groups of eight or more, individuals sense there is little "air time" for them to contribute, and they begin to occupy their time in other ways. But once you recognize the importance of size, you can choose ways to structure a discussion so that even a large group of participants will stay engaged.

Many other meeting properties influence the conduct and outcomes of a group's discussion. These include the use of agendas, presentations, and seating, as well as how the leader manages discussions, time, and decisions. These are all structural variables that you can change when you are aware of them and have the right tools. As organizational consultant Marvin Weisbord once told me, *meeting structure is anything that is directly under your control, including time, task, space, and who gets invited to participate.*[i]

You can see the influence of structure from your own experience of how a discussion changes when a group addresses some subject at the office as compared to at a restaurant. In the office, the senior manager takes her usual place at the head of the table and others take their seats along the sides. The meeting begins as the leader sets the agenda and the discussion proceeds. Now, compare this to a meeting over dinner with that same manager. Participants sit around a table where everyone can see each other. The conversation begins with participants providing some personal updates. They share a meal together. There are side conversations. Everyone has a chance to speak. When the subject for discussion is introduced, the exchange is different because various aspects of the structure have changed, and the results are likely to be different as well.

Working with Structure

Over the years, many managers have approached me with their meeting challenges. Here are some examples:

- Jane struggled to keep a team of 12 people engaged in the work of the meeting.

- Brian's meetings were often inconclusive as several members always came down on different sides of an issue.

- John's meetings produced few lasting agreements. Decisions reached in one meeting were revisited in a later meeting.

- Susan's meetings ran overtime and still didn't get everything done.

These leaders were unaware that different meeting structures could help. For example, Jane could choose either to limit meeting size or to plan specific opportunities for everyone to share their comments within the time available. Brian could choose to adopt a process to hear diverse views without derailing the discussion. John could build greater commitment to decisions by clarifying his expectations of how the group would reach a decision. And Susan could improve her meetings' timeliness by making changes in how she managed the time available. This book contains the tools I used to help them all address their challenges.

Brian's Case

Let's take a closer look at how Brian began making specific choices about meeting structure and implemented those choices using a few simple tools.

Brian's team included nine members. He told me that three of his participants seemed to have a lot to say on any subject while others held back. His meetings often ran overtime and didn't build the kind of decisions and alignment he wanted. Much of the time he hoped to achieve consensus, but found himself having to make unilateral decisions for the sake of efficiency.

Throughout the book tool names appear in **bold**. Tools are defined briefly in the text or as a side note the first time they are mentioned.

I was able to attend several of Brian's meetings. I saw that discussions continued with varying levels of interaction until there were no further comments or they ran out of time. Brian would then summarize what he believed the decision was and check for any further comments. By now, people were usually ready to move on and it was hard to tell whether there was any shared commitment to the decision.

When I met with Brian, I suggested that he reconsider how he wanted to involve the group in decision-making, and I referred him to the tool I call **Five Cs.** I also suggested he choose a structure for discussions. I recommended he select from the tools I call **1-2-All**, **Three Reaction Questions**, and **Go-Around** to create such a structure.

Below is an overview of each tool and how each could support a more effective structure in Brian's situation. The *Tool Chest* at the end of this book contains full descriptions of all these tools.

Five Cs is a tool for reviewing and selecting among the ways of making a decision with a group: **Consensus**, **Consent**, **Compromise**, **Counting** (voting), and **Consulting.** I suspected that Brian's team was not clear about his expectations for their involvement in decision-making. Some of his team may have felt they were just providing input to something that was Brian's decision to make. Others may have felt it was majority rule and they had to convince others to "win," or just give up and go along. Clarifying his intent when introducing specific discussions could help Brian set a better structure for the group's work. Depending on the situation, he could also use tools I call **Consensus Guidelines**, **Multi-Voting** and **Forces Review**.

1-2-All is a tool that provides a simple process to improve how participants share their thoughts. To use it, Brian could ask participants to reflect on the subject under consideration and make a few notes. (This is "**1**.") Brian would then ask everyone to turn to the person beside him/her to share their thoughts. (This is "**2**.") After these pairs have shared, the whole group discussion begins when Brian asks the pairs to share a key point from their discussions. He can then ask everyone for comments on what they have learned from listening to each other and move towards a conclusion. (This is "**All**.") Through this process, participants can organize their thoughts and review them with another person. It means that all get to speak on the topic. The group's time is easily managed and used efficiently. I also suggested that Brian change the usual seating pattern to create a better mix of viewpoints in any small group discussions around the table. (See another tool I call **Seating Arrangements** for more on this.)

Three Reaction Questions is a way to get more balanced reactions to some proposal and slow the tendency to focus on the "negatives." Specifically, after some plan or decision is proposed, Brian could ask the group to address three questions:

1. *"What do you like about this plan?"*

2. *"Where do you need more information?"*

3. *"Where do you have concerns?"*

He can ask the group to discuss their replies in small groups first (i.e., **1-2-All**) and then take answers to the three questions, one at a time, beginning with the first. In this way, everyone hears what they like before focusing on the questions and concerns.

Go-Around involves giving each person a brief turn to speak to the topic without interruption. Brian would introduce this by saying that he'd like everyone to take turns speaking to the point of the discussion and set a specific amount of time for each person's comments—usually a minute or two is enough. He should explain that no one should speak twice before everyone has spoken once, as this is not the time for any back-and-forth debate.

Consensus Guidelines lays out two approaches you can use to reach consensus decisions. You can use either one or both in combination.

Multi-Voting is a technique in which participants place colored, self-adhesive dots on a list showing various elements of some decision. Once all the dots are in place, the whole group reviews the pattern created and draws various conclusions.

Forces Review is a process to help you lead a group through a balanced consideration of various forces affecting achievement of some goal. It produces a range of ideas on possible actions for working with these forces.

Implementing the Changes

Brian began to introduce the changes he felt most comfortable making. He particularly wanted to be clearer about involving the group in decisions. He realized that sometimes he was asking for individual consent to go along with some decision, even though he might not get full support for all aspects of that choice. He recognized that it was better to get explicit consent than assume consensus just because no one spoke against it. At other times, Brian wanted the group's input but would reserve the right to make the final decision. Brian knew that he would need to explain his specific intent for any given discussion.

The next team meeting focused on changes to work schedules that would affect different parts of the organization. Brian explained the proposed schedule changes and then asked everyone to take a moment to consider what this would mean for his/her part of the organization. After a few minutes he asked them to discuss their reactions with the person beside them using the **Three Reaction Questions**. After a few more minutes, he reconvened the whole group. He began by asking each pair to share what they liked about the plan and then he went around again to hear questions and concerns. This first use of **1-2-All** went well. What might have become a difficult exchange between a few participants became a balanced sharing of everyone's thoughts. As he ended the discussion, Brian explained that he wanted to get their consent to this new plan. He explained what he meant by "consent" and conducted a **Go-Around** to see if he had it. In this process he made one further adjustment to his plan to get everyone's consent. In a short period of time, he had built broad understanding and agreement with the new policy.[ii]

Using This Book

Leading Great Meetings is designed as a handbook for improving any meeting where you want to accomplish some task(s) through group discussion. The first chapters introduce the choices and tools for planning, conducting and achieving results from your meetings. There are 12 structural choices and 32 tools to help you implement these choices. A separate section addresses the choices and tools for running more effective virtual meetings. There is also a chapter with suggestions for how you might begin to change your meetings. Later chapters provide examples of how a structural approach looks in practice, including "blueprints" for common meeting situations and responses to emergency situations. All the individual tools are described in full in the "Tool Chest" at the end of the book.

I have used these choices and tools many times to help leaders improve their meetings. The results have been very positive. For example, after making just a few structural changes in how one board ran its meetings, this board president commented:

> *"Your suggestions, following our discussion for the agenda, were very helpful and proved to be most effective with the board members. The attendees felt included throughout the meeting and left energized. I kind of marvel at how well the discussion went, and so easily. The approach was really a no-brainer, yet we'd never done anything like it before."*

You may want to read through the whole book, or focus only on certain areas for now. You can return to particular points when you are ready to put them to use. Even addressing just one or two choices and employing a few tools can improve many meetings.

Summary of Choices and Tools for Creating Effective Structures

There are 12 basic structural choices you can consider in planning and running a meeting. Various meeting tools are designed to help you implement these choices. These tools provide activities, processes, or guidance to establish a specific structure.

On the following pages is an overview of the choices with their supporting tools. Some tools are mentioned more than once, as they support more than one choice. Tool acronyms are defined the first time they are listed. Some tools also have special versions for use with virtual meetings and this is indicated with a superscript: **"VM"**.

Planning Choices

Six Choices in Planning	Supporting Tools
1 How you define the work of the meeting. Individuals engage each other more effectively when they share a common understanding of the purpose.	**FATT:** Defining a clear meeting task–**F**ocused, **A**ctionable, **T**imely, **T**imed.
2 Who gets invited. Discussions can lead to more insightful and effective decisions when they include a range of participants with relevant information and experience.	**ARE IN**: Identifying who should be present. **Diagonal Slice**: Selecting participants to represent the whole organization.
3 How you design the discussion. Having considered who should be present, you need to plan to involve everyone in a productive conversation. There are various factors to consider including group size, viewpoints, and presentations.	**1-2-All**: Effective engagement for groups of any size. **Four Responsibilities, Five Responsibilities**[VM]: Sharing the work of running the meeting. **Go-Around, Go-Around**[VM]: Hearing from everyone present. **PALPaR:** Creating a respectful exchange in response to some proposal.[iii] **Presentations In Perspective (PIP)**: Ensuring that presentations support discussion. **Positive Story Sharing (PSS)**: Creating conditions for dialogue. **Seating Arrangements**: Changing interaction by changing seating. **Visible Note Taking, Visible Note Taking**[VM]: Recording the progress of the group's discussion.

4 How you intend to reach decisions.

An effective discussion should build alignment and commitment to decisions. You can make this possible by choosing how you want to reach a decision and structuring the meeting to reflect your desired approach.

80/20 Principle: Clarifying agreements.

Consensus Guidelines: Reaching consensus decisions effectively and efficiently.

Five Cs: Choosing how to decide–**C**onsensus, **C**onsent, **C**ompromise, **C**ount, **C**onsult.

5 How you plan to "spend" meeting time.

There are three common weaknesses in how we plan for meeting time: ignoring the number of people who may want to comment, relying on whole group discussion, and not having a method for managing time during the meeting. Different structural techniques can help you avoid these weaknesses.

Time Planning Tips, Time Planning Tips[VM]: Planning and managing a scarce resource.

6 How you arrange the meeting space.

Physical surroundings affect the way a group talks together. You can improve many meetings by choosing to implement a setting that supports better discussions.

Circle Up: Supporting dialogue with the right physical structure.

Meeting Room Checklist, Meeting "Room" Checklist[VM]: Providing a physical setting to support the meeting.

Hybrid Meeting Checklist[VM]: Planning physical arrangements for meetings with both local and virtual participants.

Seating Arrangements: Changing interaction by changing seating.

Using the results of this planning to create the agenda.

Having made various planning choices, you can build an agenda that summarizes and communicates your design for participants.

STARS agenda: Creating one plan to manage all–**S**pecific, **T**imed, **A**ctionable, **R**elevant, **S**hared.

Conducting Choices

Four Choices While Conducting	Supporting Tools
1 How you share responsibility. Many leaders try to fill many roles: timekeeper, facilitator, discussion-leader and note taker. Taking on this many roles can be ineffective. Instead, you can share these responsibilities.	Four Responsibilities, Five Responsibilities^{VM} Visible Note Taking, Visible Note Taking^{VM}
2 How you support productive conversations. A respectful exchange of ideas can improve the quality of the group's decisions. There are a number of tools you can use to provide a structure for a productive discussion.	1-2-All 80/20 Principle Go-Around, Go-Around^{VM} **Forces Review**: Thinking constructively about both sides of an idea. **Multi-Voting**: Showing patterns of preference. PALPaR **Positive Story Sharing**: Building understanding of common experiences. **Three Reaction Questions**[iv]: Gathering balanced feedback. Visible Note Taking, Visible Note Taking^{VM}
3 How you manage time. Using time well may mean revising your plans during the meeting. There are various steps you can take to manage time effectively even in the midst of a meeting.	FATT Four Responsibilities, Five Responsibilities^{VM} Time Planning Tips, Time Planning Tips^{VM} **Time Renegotiation**: Keeping everyone responsible for managing time.
4 How you work with any conflict. Differing views help expand and test the group's thinking, but they can also create unproductive conflict. Various tools can help you maintain a respectful exchange, and minimize defensive behaviors.	1-2-All Forces Review **Future Focus**: Working on the desired future rather than past problems. PALPaR Three Reaction Questions

Two Choices for Achieving Results	Supporting Tools
1 How you build decisions. Decisions can be built a step at a time to respect and incorporate various views and align people around the conclusions.	FATT **80/20 Principle** **Affinity Grouping**: Visualizing relationships among ideas. **Consensus Guidelines** **Five Cs** **Multi-Voting**
2 How you follow up. Meeting outcomes can be implemented effectively and consistently when people plan their actions and reflect on subsequent results in an appropriate follow-up conversation.	**Follow-Up Timing**: Choosing the best time to learn from actions. **Three Follow-Up Questions**: Learning from a balanced review of progress.

Achieving Results Choices

Part I

Planning the Structure of Your Meeting

I have learned over and over again the benefit of taking time to plan some upcoming meeting. Once upon a time, my planning might have consisted of arranging a time and place to meet and preparing some "agenda" of topics to be discussed. What else was necessary? After all, everyone "knows how" to meet.

This lack of attention to any real planning leads to the frustrating experiences many of us have in meetings. Discussions go around in circles, some people dominate, and the eventual decision may be unclear or poorly supported. Such meetings lead some people to advocate for doing away with meetings altogether. Yet, a meeting is a critical leadership tool. Meetings are a great way to build insights and alignment into an organization.

By taking time to plan, you can be the architect of your meetings and design a structure that will help you run a reliably successful session. Such planning does not have to take a lot of time, but it means considering a few choices affecting the structure of your meeting that you may not have considered in the past.

There are six choices you can make to plan the structure for your meeting:

1) How you define the work of the meeting.

2) Who gets invited.

3) How you design the discussion.

4) How you intend to reach decisions.

5) How you plan to "spend" meeting time.

6) How you arrange the meeting space.

You can improve almost any meeting by attending to even some of these choices.

The following chapters describe the nature of each choice and outline the relevant tools you can use to implement your desired structure. Each chapter includes an example of how that choice and its tools work in practice, along with an exercise you can complete to see how that choice applies in your situation.

Finally, once you have considered your choices, you can record the results in an agenda for conducting the meeting. I will explain how you create an effective public agenda (using the tool called **STARS**) in the last chapter of this section.

Chapter 1

How You Define the Work of the Meeting

What's the task to be accomplished with this group? While you may think of it simply as "the weekly staff meeting," ask yourself, "If I don't expect some tangible results, then why am I having this meeting?"

Creating an effective structure begins with clarifying your intended results. Individuals engage each other more effectively around a task when they share a common understanding of the purpose. Specifically, they are more likely to come prepared, to stay "on topic," and to use meeting time more efficiently.

Unfortunately, many meetings do not have any clear tasks for the participants to work on together. For example, a typical agenda item might be listed as "communication planning," but this is not a well-defined task. One participant may think it refers to some staff briefing while someone else thinks it refers to a new e-mail policy. Consider how much better the preparation and discussion could be if the agenda listed the intended task as:

To develop a better means of communicating quarterly results to our staff so everyone can see how this information is relevant to his/her responsibilities.

A well-defined task has four characteristics:

- **Focused:** There should be a specific topic for discussion that is clear and bounded so everyone understands exactly what is under consideration. This is the work you've called this meeting to accomplish. There can be more than one task in a meeting, and each should be clearly defined.

- **Actionable:** The work to be done can be acted on by those present (not referred to someone not present). In most cases, you don't want a theoretical discussion, but something that participants have direct personal involvement in resolving.

- **Timely:** This is the appropriate time to address this topic. It is important (and possibly urgent) that it be addressed in this meeting. While this may seem obvious, I frequently attend meetings where some part of the agenda could and should be assigned to some future meeting.

- **Timed:** A realistic amount of meeting time is assigned to complete this task given the expected discussion and number of participants.

The more clearly each agenda item has these **FATT** characteristics, the more likely it is that the group will engage effectively in the work of the meeting. A **FATT** agenda item is like a "fat pitch" in baseball—right over the plate so you can get a solid swing at it.

I sometimes get asked if all meetings need a task or decision for the group to work on together. What if you want to use your meeting to update your group about some subject? Could this meet the **FATT** criteria? Yes, an "update" can meet these criteria if it is clear what you are asking participants to do with the information. For example, the task of an update could be to confirm that all understand and will act on the information. Also, some updates involve providing information for planning actions and help the group align its efforts. But if an update is only for some status briefing, then this may be neither an effective nor efficient use of everyone's time.

Working with this Choice

Reflection. Review the specific items listed for discussion at some recent meeting that you led or attended. Consider the following:

- Were these items adequately defined so that everyone understood what needed to be discussed? Is this group able to act on the outcomes of the discussion?

- Were there any items that really didn't need to be discussed at this time? Or any tasks that didn't need to involve this whole group?

- Was there an adequate amount of time planned for the work of each main item? In hindsight, was the planned time realistic given the scope of the discussion needed?

Beginning to Make Changes. Looking forward to a coming meeting, begin applying the **FATT** criteria to how you define the work of the meeting.

- What do you need to do to clarify particular tasks you hope to accomplish? Will the intended outcome be clear to all attending?

- Can you assign an adequate amount of time to the task given the size of your group and the complexity of the decision?

Before you make a final decision about timing, look ahead to the choices and tools in chapters 3 and 5 that address how you design the discussion and plan to spend meeting time. You may also want to see the examples of specific meeting agendas and "blueprints" in chapter 14.

Chapter 2

Who Gets Invited

We often invite "the usual suspects" to our meetings. But do these people have all the necessary information and insights for an effective discussion? And are they the ones who will implement any action plans that arise from the meeting? I have been in meetings where some work cannot be completed because some people and perspectives were missing. Who is present for a discussion is a key structural choice.

For example, I once facilitated a meeting for group of non-profit leaders who needed to coordinate their fundraising efforts. It was a complex and controversial subject, but they arrived at significant new insights over the course of the day-long meeting. In closing, they agreed to try out some "experiments" with a new way of working together. Implementing these ideas required the development of a plan and communication to their various staffs around the country. This action was assigned to two people who were not at the meeting and did not have the context of the discussion. Partially as a result of their abscence, the intended actions never were completed and the time and expense of that meeting were lost.

You can plan to lead to more insightful and effective decisions by including a range of participants with relevant information and experience. A group makes wiser decisions when it has some diversity of views along with the ability to share these views.[v] After the meeting, such a varied group of participants also improves the likelihood that any decisions or actions will be implemented.

There are two tools that can help you think through who should be present. One way to identify participants with a range of information and stake in some discussion is to invite those who **ARE IN** as they have:

- **A**uthority to act
- **R**esources relevant to the task
- **E**xpertise
- **I**nformation
- **N**eed, as they will be impacted by the decision

ARE IN was defined by Weisbord and Janoff (2007, 17). They view this tool as a way to ensure you get the "whole system" in your meeting. However, **ARE IN** is still helpful if you are running a meeting that doesn't require representatives of the whole system. It provides a great set of criteria for checking that you are including all the necessary people to accomplish some particular meeting task.

Diagonal Slice is another tool you can use to identify participants. It suggests you invite participants from a range of organizational levels and functions across a "diagonal slice" of the organization. Note that this tool does not presume any particular number of participants. You may be able to have a representative slice of the organization by including only a few more people than you might have otherwise. The insights from different perspectives, particularly from those responsible for the delivery of some service to your clients or customers, can be very valuable. See the *Tool Chest* for more information on both tools.

Don't forget that you can invite additional participants for only that part of the meeting where their involvement is most appropriate. Put the task at the beginning of the agenda, and excuse them when it is done. I've never known anyone to complain about being given the opportunity to leave a meeting when its subject was no longer relevant.

Working with This Choice

Reflection. Review some recent meeting.

- Did the participants have all the necessary information for the work of the meeting?
- Was everyone present who had to follow up on any actions identified?

- Did you have people at the meeting simply because they usually attend? Would it have been OK not to invite them—with an explanation, of course?

- How many additional participants would you have needed to ensure you had a representative sample of your organization or system?

Consider which people you need for some upcoming discussion. Who do you want to participate by name, or by perspective?

Beginning to Make Changes. Add several additional/different people to your next meeting as relevant to the work of that session. See how the discussion changes.

You will probably need to explain why you invited the additional participants. In addition, you should plan some way to make the discussion comfortable and respectful for everyone, particularly as you want to hear from those who are not regular participants in your meetings. See the next chapter for more on how to do this.

Chapter 3

How You Design the Discussion

Having considered who should be present at your meeting, you should plan how you will involve everyone in a productive conversation. There are five factors to consider:

- Group size
- "Strangers"
- Viewpoints
- Outspoken individuals
- Presentations

One or more of these factors is likely to be present in any meeting. Each of them can be addressed through the way you structure your discussion, and there are various tools to help you do this.

Group Size

If you have eight or more participants, you need to create a structure for discussion so all can participate fully. With a larger group, some participants will find it hard to contribute. By the time they do get to speak, what they intended to say may no longer feel relevant. In these situations, it is natural for some participants to disengage. However, you can keep everyone involved by creating opportunities for small group discussion using the process laid out by the tool **1-2-All**. Each person gets to speak in a small group, and that discussion is then summarized in a report back to the whole group. Such a structure can be set up quickly without changing rooms or chairs and done in ways that manage time efficiently. It can seem like a very natural process, which in fact it is.

1-2-All stands for its process: "**1**" for individual reflection, "**2**" for sharing reactions with at least one other person, and "**All**" for the final sharing of reactions and conclusions with the whole group.

For example, in the introduction, I shared the story of how Brian resolved some of his meeting challenges. After presenting a proposed change, he simply asked everyone to take a moment to consider what this would mean for his/her part of the organization. After several minutes he then asked them to discuss their reactions with a neighbor. After a few more minutes, he reconvened the whole group and asked each pair to share the key points from their discussion. Finally, once all had reported, he asked everyone what they were learning and then conducted a **Go-Around** to determine their consent to the proposal.

"Strangers" and Status Differences

Go-Around involves giving each person a brief turn to speak to the topic, without interruption or comments as everyone else simply listens.

Research has shown that productive, respectful conversation is more likely when we accept each other as individuals who have similarities as human beings and have common experiences as we work, think, and respond to situations.[vi] This is particularly important when some participants don't know others well or they differ in role, responsibilities, age, gender, or race. You need to lower the barriers to more open conversation by choosing a structure that helps participants relate to each other. At a minimum you should make sure all get an equal chance to speak and be heard early in the meeting. **Go-Around** provides a good way to do this. Using **Seating Arrangements** may also help you avoid creating some power dynamics based on where people sit.

A more powerful approach involves building some appreciation of common experience through sharing stories. In this case, story sharing should be relevant to the work to be done, enable all to be heard, and build on positive experiences.

Seating Arrangements is a tool for creating a more even exchange among participants by planning seating to give all a "good" seat at the table no matter their status, and to avoid the impression that one area is where the power and influence reside.

One simple and effective way to do this is to ask people to interview each other in pairs about some positive past experience with an aspect of the topic under consideration. Key themes from these interviews are then summarized for the whole group. The process is similar to **1-2-All,** except that there is a structured interview process between pairs of participants. Specifically, one person takes on the role of interviewer and asks the following:

- *"Tell me about a time when you felt very good about your success with (the topic under consideration)."*
- *"What happened? Who was involved?"*
- *"What made this so successful?"*

The pair change roles and the process is repeated. When the interviews are complete, the whole group reconvenes and shares what they heard from each other. See **Positive Story Sharing** in the *Tool Chest* for more on how to do this.

Viewpoints

Some people will be reticent to speak to a group that they know includes people with more authority or different views. You will need to create a structure to help everyone participate.

A simple way to do this is by providing opportunities for people to speak in small groups, mixing participants by views and status. **1-2-All** is helpful here. Other tools you can use include **Go-Around, PALPaR, Positive Story Sharing**, and **Seating Arrangements.**

Outspoken Individuals

Some groups contain people who dominate any discussion. They speak forcefully on a subject and "hijack" the direction of subsequent contributions. Other participants may remain silent or focus on their reactions to the first individual. The breadth of possible comments may be lost.

Tools like **Go-Around, 1-2-All**, and **PALPaR** provide structures that enable more balanced contributions. **1-2-All** is particularly helpful in that the outspoken individual is now speaking to a small group with less influence on what others are sharing. By beginning with individual reflection, **1-2-All** also enables everyone to gather his/her thoughts before speaking, which can be important when there is an individual who thinks out loud and is always ready with an opinion.

See chapter 15 for an example of how **PALPaR** was used to build a productive conversation among a group with varying viewpoints and some outspoken individuals in a meeting that was operating under Parliamentary Procedure (a.k.a. "Robert's Rules of Order").

Presentations

Presentations create their own challenges for productive conversations. Many meetings are intended to involve everyone in discussions after a presentation sets out the key points. However, participant engagement usually declines after 15 minutes or so of listening to someone speak if there is no opportunity for real interaction. We seem to become "students" again and passive listeners to the lecture.

Positive Story Sharing enables individuals to reflect and share stories of positive past personal experiences in some aspect of the work of this meeting.

PALPaR is a process for gathering feedback on some proposal or plan in a way that supports reflection and listening to any feedback before responding. The acronym summarizes the process: **P**resent, **A**sk, **L**isten, **P**ause, and **R**eply.

Try to keep presentations brief and interactive. Plan ahead to create a more engaging structure for any presentation through such simple techniques as telling participants what they should be prepared to discuss after they hear the presentation, or by keeping presentations short. The tool I call **PIP** (**Presentations In Perspective**) gives guidelines for using presentations to support more effective discussion.

Preparing Your Structure in Advance to Support Discussion

You should plan a structure to address any or all of these factors in advance of the meeting. Even the risk of an outspoken individual may be anticipated if you know your group well. Selecting several tools to create a structure for your discussion will also give you more insight into how much time you need to allow for a given agenda item. (See chapter 5 for more on planning meeting time).

I also find it helpful to look ahead to how I will conduct the meeting, to anticipate any additional tools I may need to maintain productive discussions. See chapter 9, *How You Support Productive Conversations*, for ideas on additional tools for different situations.

PIP (Presentations In Perspective) is a set of guidelines for placing presentations in the context of the work of a meeting to support more effective discussion.

Working with This Choice

Reflection. During your next meeting observe how different people participate in discussions. Are several voices more dominant than others? Does discussion seem to go back and forth between two or three individuals with little interaction or acknowledgement of others? Do some people always speak first? Do some make very few contributions? How would you like to see this pattern of discussion change?

Beginning to Make Changes. Choose one of the five factors above for specific attention as you plan a future meeting. Do you want to do something to address group size, the presence of "strangers" or status differences, differing viewpoints, outspoken individuals, or the role of presentations?

For Additional Support. You will find examples of the use of these tools in different situations on my blog at **www.meetingfor-results.com/blog**.

Chapter 4

How You Intend to Reach Decisions

Effective discussions can build commitment to decisions, but many meetings fail to do this. One reason for this can be participant assumptions about the nature of the decision. For example, participants may assume they are providing input to the leader's decision. Meanwhile, the leader assumes s/he is gaining their commitment to the decision. You may have had this experience when a leader asks the group in closing if there are any other comments on some pending decision. Hearing none, the leader presumes s/he has everyone's support and moves on. But is this really the case? A decision that seems to have the group's support may not have everyone's commitment as participants assume it is the leader's decision to make.[vii]

Another reason for ineffective group decision-making is the use of an approach that doesn't fit the situation. For example, choosing to reach a decision by voting doesn't work well when you want to build alignment and support—voting always risks creating winners and losers.

You can minimize these difficulties by choosing the best approach to making a decision with your group for a given situation and conducting the meeting to reflect that approach. There are five basic ways to involve a group in making a decision. I refer to these as the **Five Cs**. Each is appropriate in certain situations.

- **Consensus:** Everyone truly supports the decision.
- **Consent:** Everyone supports the decision as "good enough."

- **Compromise:** Each person gives up something to reach a decision.
- **Count** (votes): The "side" with the most votes wins the decision.
- **Consult:** The leader wants the group's input, but makes the final decision.

The approach to decision-making you choose will affect how you structure the discussion. I summarize the nature of each approach below, and you can find more information in the description of the **Five Cs** in the *Tool Chest*.

Consensus

True consensus decisions are ones for which everyone involved has clearly indicated his or her support. If one person has an objection, then you don't have consensus. Consensus decision-making does not mean that everyone has agreed to *all* aspects of the proposed decision. Areas that fail to gain everyone's support can be set aside as "not yet agreed" while action begins on the areas where there is consensus.[viii] Refer to the tools **Consensus Guidelines** and **80/20 Principle** for further assistance.

Consent

A decision by consent is more flexible than one by consensus. It enables each participant to give his/her explicit, if qualified, support. While some individuals may be fully behind the decision, others may support it to the extent that they have no *fundamental* objection to the decision.[ix] This is not the same as decision by *implied* consent or decision by exception, where it is assumed to be OK to proceed if no one speaks up. In a consent decision, each person explicitly agrees to the overall decision having clarified any limits or exceptions to his/her support.

Compromise

In a compromise, each "side" gives up something they want in order to achieve support for the overall agreement. It is a negotiation. This can be one of the hardest decisions to achieve and so groups sometimes resort to voting or relying on an implied consent instead.

Consensus Guidelines provides ways to achieve a decision that all support. This tool provides two ways to achieve consensus with a group.

80/20 Principle highlights the tendency for groups to put much of their energy into discussing areas of disagreement, and ignoring broader areas of agreement. Groups subsequently fail to give attention to the majority of the subject on which they do agree and where forward progress is possible. This tool makes this tendency visible and asks the group to focus on the 80% to begin.

Counting

Counting the number of votes for or against a proposal is a common means of group decision-making. However, this approach is poorly suited for building broad alignment and support for some decision. It has two weaknesses. First, it creates a form of group pressure to go along with the majority. And second, the "losers" can always say, *"Don't blame me, I didn't vote for it."* Of course, voting can be efficient, and it is useful when a formal record of the decision is required.

Consult

The fifth means of group decision-making is to be explicit about leaving the final decision with one person, usually the person with overall accountability. In this situation, the group is being consulted for their views. Participants typically recognize the different levels of authority for some decision and appreciate being consulted on their views before the decision is made. The tool I call **PALPaR** is particularly helpful for this approach to decision-making.

Working with This Choice

Reflection. Consider some recent decisions you made with your group in a meeting. How were those decisions reached? Do you think everyone understood how you were to decide? Did you use implied consent or assume consensus as long as no one spoke up when you brought the discussion to a close?

For more insight into how groups reach (poor) decisions and what can be done about this, see *Wiser: Getting Beyond Groupthink to Make Groups Smarter* by Cass Sunstein and Reid Hastie.

Beginning to Make Changes. How could decisions you share with your group be handled using another one of the **Five Cs**? Look ahead to some upcoming discussion and see if you can clarify in advance how you would like the group to contribute to any particular decision. Would this represent a change in how some would assume any decision was usually made? If so, plan to briefly explain how you'd like the group to be involved this time in decision making.

Chapter 5

How You Plan to "Spend" Meeting Time

Meetings are often criticized as a waste of time. This may be due to their lack of results, but it may also be due to poor time management. Many of us fail to "spend" meeting time like the scarce resource it is.

There are three common weaknesses in allocating meeting time:

- Unrealistic timing
- Reliance on whole group discussion
- Time inflation

Unrealistic Timing

Many meetings run over time or don't accomplish everything on the agenda. I can often predict these difficulties simply by looking at the agenda. Is the time assigned to various items realistic given the group's size and the intended discussion? An agenda with "five minutes" planned for a discussion with a group of ten participants is hardly enough time for all to speak. If the intent isn't to give all a chance for input, why put it on the agenda as a discussion?

Reliance on Whole Group Discussion

This may be the single most common weakness in how most meetings spend time. Assuming that a meeting is one long whole group discussion presumes that everyone can participate in that one conversation for the duration of the meeting. This is a very inefficient use of time. You can improve the effective use of meeting time through small group discussions that enable you to double up on the use of time through parallel conversations. Small group work also keeps participants engaged in the work since everyone gets more air time. Such small group discussions can be set up simply, right in the meeting room, at one table. See the tool **1-2-All** for how to do this.

Time Inflation

Time inflation occurs when discussions are allowed to expand to fill the time available and then some. This often happens when the meeting is conducted as one continuous whole group discussion. I recommend you plan to spend the time necessary to get the results you want, choose an appropriate structure for the discussion, and then conduct the meeting to spend the time you planned and nothing more.

The tool I call **Time Planning Tips** contains various ideas to help you structure meeting time wisely. **Four Responsibilities** explains the roles you can share with meeting participants to help keep the discussion on track and on time. Finally, the **Time Renegotiation** tool can be used to help you make adjustments to time or agenda with participants during the meeting itself.

Working with This Choice

Reflection. Looking at a recent agenda, do you have many "five minute" items? Was this realistic? Did the meeting accomplish its intended outcomes in the planned time? What else affected your timing?

Beginning to Make Changes. Revise the timing in your next meeting. This may mean you need to put fewer items on the agenda, perhaps by removing "updates" and focusing only on the items that require real discussion. Consider a minimum of two minutes per person for any given discussion. Add more time if the subject is complex or controversial. Make some specific decisions about the structure of your discussion (chapter 3) and then assign the time required. Ask someone to be the timekeeper (as defined in **Four Responsibilities**) on key discussions and use **Time Renegotiation** if you go over time on an item.

Participants arriving late can often cause a loss of time. Is there some agenda item, like a check-in using **Go-Around**, that you could put at the beginning? This can serve two purposes: It gets everyone participating and allows for the fact that someone may arrive late.

Time Planning Tips is a collection of practices for more reliably and productively structuring the use of time in meetings.

Four Responsibilities describes the four responsibilities that need to be filled to varying degrees for a more effective meeting. These responsibilities can be shared.

Time Renegotiation is a practice for openly involving participants in the reallocation of available time when meeting demands change the original plan.

Chapter 6

How You Arrange the Meeting Space

Different physical settings support or hinder discussions. We are affected by the subtle signals a space "gives off." Consider how a discussion differs when held around a table in a coffee shop as compared to a traditional conference room. The surroundings of many coffee shops imply that this is a place for a free exchange of ideas among friends and associates. The surroundings of many conference rooms imply authority and responsibility and a more limited exchange of views.

Here are some of the physical characteristics that I give particular attention to in arranging meeting space:

- A circular table enables everyone to see each other and gives a sense of equal standing. A rectangular table implies hierarchy and people tend to sit in relationship to the leader at the "head." I try to avoid such a table if possible.

- A podium, fixed mike, or computer and projector all send a message of who has the power, and this may not support the desired discussion.

- Chairs that can be rearranged easily are helpful when you want the group to work in sub-groups by pulling two or three chairs together.

- Windows and daylight are important for maintaining group energy.

- A room that supports visible, ongoing note taking on white boards or flip charts enables everyone to see the group's work as it proceeds.

Three tools can help you choose the best space, or find a way to better match the physical structure to your meeting's purpose:

- **Circle Up**
- **Meeting Room Checklist**
- **Seating Arrangements**.

Circle Up suggests ways to arrange your meeting space in a circle, or as close to a circle as you can get. Even a square table is better than a rectangle. Sometimes, it may be better to have no table at all. I once helped a leader conduct a difficult meeting in a board-room with a long, massive table. To improve the discussion on this difficult topic, we set up a circle of chairs with a flip chart at one side of the room. We ignored the table for meeting together until we had lunch, at which time we sat at the table...until we were ready to resume work. The discussion went better than any-one had anticipated.

Meeting Room Checklist provides a set of requirements for a healthy meeting space, one that is more likely to support good, engaged conversation.

Seating Arrangements asks you to consider how participants, including the leader, are seated and choose an arrangement that supports good engagement, dialogue, and decision making.

Working with This Choice

Reflection. Where do you sit at meetings you lead? Do you take the same seat each time? Is it at the head of the table? Where do others sit? Do they usually take the same seats? Is there some sub-group of attendees that always sits together?

Beginning to Make Changes. A simple action is to take a different seat yourself and see how this works for you. Do the interactions change? If someone asks why you changed your seat, you can explain that you thought it might change the discussion if you didn't take "parent" seat at the head of the table. Also consider moving your meeting to a space that fulfills more of the sugges-tions in the **Meeting Room Checklist** and see how this feels for you and your participants.

Chapter 7

One Plan to Manage All

Having worked with some or all of the choices above, you can build an agenda for a meeting structured to achieve your desired results. I recommend that drafting an agenda be one of the last things you do in preparing for the meeting so that it reflects the planning choices you've made. Unfortunately, many people substitute creating an agenda for more careful planning.

When you are ready to prepare the agenda, the tool I call **STARS** helps you build one to assist you and the participants in holding your meeting. The tool's name is an acronym that stands for five properties of an effective agenda:

- **S**pecific: Points to be covered are explicitly defined. This definition should provide a clear focus and expected action to be taken—in other words, a **FATT** statement of purpose for each main agenda item.

- **T**imed: Each part of the agenda has an assigned period of time reflecting the nature of the discussion and number of participants.

- **A**ctionable: Each point of the agenda should inform or lead to some action by those present.

- **R**elevant: The topic should be relevant to everyone present. If it is only relevant to a few, there may be some other way to address these points outside the meeting or to have some people join only for that part of the meeting that pertains to them.

- **Shared** in advance: For most meetings, participants should have an opportunity to see an agenda 24 to 48 hours in advance in order to prepare.

I recommend that you begin by organizing the agenda around the key task(s) of the meeting and then add other items like introductions, updates, and so on. If you have more than one task to address, try to place the most important or difficult task near the beginning of the meeting to make sure it gets the attention it deserves.

Agendas: Before and After

I want to show you two different agendas for the same committee meeting so you can see the impact of more careful planning. On the following pages are examples of an agenda for a committee that had struggled to get things done and stay on time in its meetings.

The first agenda shows the original plan for an upcoming meeting. It's an example of what their agendas had usually looked like. Fortunately, I had a chance to meet with the committee chairman before the meeting and help him revise his agenda.

The second agenda shows how the same meeting's agenda looked after making various decisions to create a structure to serve the results they wanted to achieve in the time they had. It is an example of a **STARS** agenda with one exception—I have added italicized explanations under "comments" in a side column to highlight the various structural choices. *These explanations would not have been part of the actual agenda and are included here to help you see the logic of the design.*

The second agenda also contains a variety of information for participants to help the meeting go as intended. Specifically, this includes some timing details like "one minute each" for a check-in, or specific timing for various activities in the main discussion item (on Transition Towns). You want participants to understand the questions and the process of any discussion along with the time available to do so. Writing them down in the agenda gives everyone the "road map" for the meeting and limits the need for questions about process.

Agenda *(before)*

Introductions	5 minutes
Approval of December 10 Minutes	2 minutes
Review of Agenda	5 minutes

- Identification of minutes taker and timekeeper

Use of External Facilitator	10 minutes
Update on 350 Brainstorming Initiative	10 minutes
Winter and Spring Community Education Programs Updates	50 minutes
Transition Town Initiative Planning[x]	5 minutes

- Reactions to last month's presentation
- Planning for implementing first two steps, including leadership of those steps

Plan for February Meeting	5 minutes

Agenda *(after)*

Comments	Time	Agenda
Pre-determined roles.	NA	Timekeeper: HE Minutes: MM
Several small items grouped together to better manage time.	7:00-7:20 [20 min]	**Introductions, minutes, agenda** • Introductions • Check-in [1 minute each] • Approval of meeting minutes from last time • Review of tonight's agenda
One of main purposes has been moved up in the agenda to make sure it gets its full time for discussion. *Information is reviewed in small groups using **Three Reaction Questions** as committee is large (12) and there is much to consider.*	7:20 – 8:20 [60 min]	**Transition Town initiative decision** 1) Review summary of the proposed design of the 12 step program presented last month. [10 minutes] 2) Break into 3 groups for discussion of specific steps. [15 minutes] Questions for each group: • What do you like about these steps? • What information do you need? • What do you not like or find challenging? 3) As a whole group discuss our answers to the three questions. [20 minutes] • Identify any points needing more information 4) Decision: Do we want to support this initiative? [15 minutes] • If so, how should we begin? • Who will lead the initial steps?
As a discussion and decision item, this needed more time and clearer purpose.	8:20 – 8:35 [15 min]	**Decision on using external facilitator** 1) Report from subcommittee who met with facilitator. 2) Discussion: What additional questions do we have as a committee about the need/role of a facilitator? How will we address these? 3) Decision: Shall we ask facilitator to come to our next meeting as a first step? • Want everyone's consent (or not).

8:35 – 8:45 (10 min)	Update on upcoming events Share information on 350 Brainstorming Initiative • Time, place, leadership, format, goals, response to date Update on Winter and Spring Community Education Programs so all can plan their calendars.	*Time was cut here to be used elsewhere. Information is supported by a handout.*

8:45 –
8:55
(10 min)
	Wrap up
	   • Actions this month
	   • Topics for next meeting agenda
	   • Feedback on this meeting
		More time added to make clearer the expectation for the wrap up.

Working with Your Agenda

Reflection. Review the agenda for some recent meeting that you led or attended. Consider the following:

- How far in advance was the agenda shared with participants? Did everyone come prepared?

- How many discrete items for discussion were on this agenda? Was it realistic to include them all?

- Were items adequately defined so that everyone understood what needed to be discussed? Were all items relevant and actionable for those present?

- Were there any items that really didn't need to be discussed at this time? Did any items get moved to some future agenda as the time in this meeting ran out?

- Were there any items that didn't need to involve this whole group?

- Were there any updates or reports on this agenda? If so, was it clear what participants were to do with this information? Was sharing the information in the meeting the best and most efficient way to communicate this?

- Was there an adequate amount of time planned for the meeting? How was the time actually spent? In hindsight, was the planned time realistic given the scope of the discussion needed?

Beginning to Make Changes. Review the examples of specific meeting agendas and "blueprints" in chapter 14. Then begin making improvements wherever it seems easiest. Maybe this is by providing clearer timing for different items. Or maybe this means removing some items from the agenda that don't involve everyone. Or maybe it is simply getting the agenda to participants in advance of the meeting.

Part II

Structural Choices for Conducting Your Meeting

Having made some choices to plan your meeting, you already have a much stronger structure for conducting it. As the meeting proceeds, however, you may encounter circumstances that require you to make additional choices to create an effective structure in the moment. This section presents four choices that may arise as you lead your meeting and introduces the tools you can use to support you. The four choices are:

1) How you share responsibility.

2) How you support productive conversations.

3) How you manage time.

4) How you work with conflict.

I recommend that you review these choices and tools as you plan your meeting. Knowing your participants and the work to be done, you may be able to anticipate the need to address some of these choices for conducting the meeting. You can select some relevant tools and have them ready to use, if needed, as you run the session.

Looking ahead, Part III will present two additional choices you should consider to help you achieve results through well-supported decisions and effective follow up. You may want to keep these additional choices in mind as you conduct the meeting. The two final choices as you work to achieve results are:

1) How you build decisions.

2) How you follow up.

Chapter 8

How You Share Responsibility

Many leaders try to do it all in the meetings they "run." I know I have been guilty of this. I try to move the group through the agenda, keep track of time, balance participation, and share my own thoughts. I may even serve as note taker for the discussion! Filling multiple roles in a meeting is tiring and ineffective. It can cause participants to take less responsibility for overall meeting success and is not good leadership practice.

You can create a more effective meeting by sharing key responsibilities for running the meeting. Individual participants are asked (or volunteer) to take on specific roles. These are temporary assignments that can rotate among participants from one topic to the next and from one meeting to another.

Weisbord and Janoff (2010, 51) suggest a set of roles that can be shared in most meetings. With some modifications, those four roles are:

- **Discussion leader:** Responsible for making sure each person who wants to speak to the subject is able to do so in the time available.

- **Timekeeper:** Keeps track of the time for each main point on the agenda. Alerts the group when the planned time on an item is running out.

- **Recorder:** Uses flip chart or white board to visibly track the progress of the group's discussion where all can see it.

- **Information manager/minutes:** Responsible for maintaining the formal documentation and recorded minutes of the group's work.[xi]

It is particularly helpful to share the role of discussion leader when you are the one with most of the information or authority for some proposal. Trying to explain your proposal and also facilitate an open dialogue is difficult at best.

Identifying volunteers to fulfill these roles is something that can be done on the spot during the meeting. The roles are not that complex. For more information, see **Four Responsibilities** in the *Tool Chest*. Share this tool with your meeting participants so they understand their responsibilities. You may also want to refer to the **Visible Note Taking** tool to clarify the responsibilities of the recorder and distinguish this from the more familiar role played by someone taking minutes.

Note: If you have a large meeting and set up several small groups to work in parallel, give **Four Responsibilities** to each small group and ask them to divide up the roles to complete their discussion. This is much more effective than trying to oversee the progress of multiple groups yourself.

Working with This Choice

Reflection. How could one or more of these four roles have helped you run a recent meeting? Is there one that is often needed, perhaps timekeeper or recorder?

Beginning to Make Changes. While you could introduce all four roles at your next meeting, you may want to begin by asking someone to take on one of the roles, perhaps that of timekeeper. Or, you could take on the role of recorder as someone else leads a discussion for his/her part of the agenda.

Visible Note Taking: This tool outlines techniques for recording real-time notes of key comments and decisions where all can see them to keep the discussion on track. The original four roles included a "reporter" and no "information manager." I have revised that role here for more general meeting use apart from the large group meetings that are the focus of Weisbord and Janoff's work.

Chapter 9

How You Support Productive Conversations

Productive conversations are those where we can contribute our thoughts and know that they have been heard and considered. We feel valued for our thoughts and gain new insights from others. Such conversation builds alignment and understanding and may improve the wisdom of group's decisions. It is essential to the effective accomplishment of much of the work in a meeting.

Many of the choices you make in planning a meeting should set the stage for more productive conversations. In particular, the third planning choice (chapter 3) focuses on considerations and tools for creating effective discussions. But as you conduct the meeting, you may need to take additional steps to ensure that you continue to support good conversation.

There are three guidelines you can use to make a productive discussion more likely:

- Give everyone a chance to speak.
- Make sure that all views receive a respectful hearing.
- Avoid situations likely to create defensive behaviors.

Give everyone a chance to speak.

At a minimum, a productive conversation requires giving an equal opportunity for each participant to speak and be heard. You may need to make sure this happens at various points in a meeting—when one or two voices are dominating the conversation or the discussion seems to be going in circles. Simply explain that you want to go around the group and give each person a chance to speak to the subject. Make it clear that you'd like each person to speak once before anyone replies or speaks a second time. See the tool **Go-Around** for more.

You may think that your group is too large or there is not enough time for everyone to speak. After all, ten people at a minute or so per person means taking ten minutes just for a round of comments. If this initial round is followed by replies and further comments, the time can quickly double. Fortunately, there is another approach that uses time efficiently in any size group. It uses the process I introduced earlier that I call **1-2-All**.

1: First give everyone a minute or so for individual reflection.

2: Ask each person to share his/her thoughts with one or two others in a small group.

All: Have the small groups report out to the whole group. One person reports for each small group.

This process supports both conversation and the development of new insights because it gives everyone a chance to speak and learn from the reactions of others in a small group. A small group may also be a safer environment for some to test their thinking. Then, when the whole group hears the summary of the small group discussions, common themes emerge. And all this happens efficiently in a defined period of time.

Make sure all views receive a respectful hearing.

Another challenge arises when someone states a different view from the rest of the group. If the person and his/her views are ignored or minimized in some way, then the opportunity for a safe, meaningful exchange is lost. While ground rules that ask people to treat each other respectfully may help, I find a structural approach is more effective since it does not require remembering how you are supposed to behave when the conversation gets difficult.

Several different tools can be used to create a more respectful discussion. I've already mentioned **Go-Around** and **1-2-All** and both can be helpful here, alone or in combination with other tools.

Another tool, that I call **PALPaR**, follows a process I learned from the work of Kathleen Dannemiller (Dannemiller Tyson, 2000). You first **Present** some proposal and **Ask** for feedback.

Then you **Listen** to the feedback without comment, simply recording the points raised where all can see (and know they have been heard). Next, you **Pause** (for a break or until the next meeting) to give yourself an opportunity to reflect on the feedback. Finally, you **Reply** to the feedback, summarizing what you heard and explaining how you have/have not taken the feedback into account in modifying your original proposal.

Here is an example of **PALPaR** in use. This leader had joined the organization about six months before and now wanted to engage his staff in his vision for the organization going forward. He called his staff together for a two-day meeting to cover various subjects. His staff came from a merger of two earlier organizations, and he wanted to do everything he could to structure a meeting to build a safe, respectful discussion. He used **PALPaR** to structure the part of the meeting that addressed his vision. On the afternoon of the first day, he presented his vision for the organization and explained he wanted their input to improve it. Next he asked everyone to turn to one or two others and discuss three questions (following **1-2-All** using a version of the **Three Reaction Questions**).

- What did they hear that they liked?
- Where did they have questions or need information?
- Where did they have concerns or see challenges?

After ten minutes, he reconvened the session and asked the small groups to summarize their discussion of the first question. As the groups reported their comments, he summarized their points (using their words) on a flip chart (i.e., **Visible Note Taking**). He then repeated the process for questions 2 and 3. This demonstrated that he was listening carefully to their comments. When he was done, he thanked them for their input and explained he wanted to think about their comments and would continue this session on the following day.

Next day, he summarized what he had learned from their feedback and proceeded to give various explanations and explained some resulting changes to his vision. He asked the group if they felt he had heard them and whether they had any further questions now. All seemed satisfied and much clearer on his direction. Later he told me that this process had helped him manage his own initial reactions to the feedback and integrate his staff's comments with his own ideas before replying.

Any use of **1-2-All** or **PALPaR** is best planned and introduced *before* some individual raises a difficult viewpoint. Like the story I just shared, you may know when some agenda item is likely to generate a variety of comments, some of which may be difficult for people to share. Both tools are implemented one step at a time at the appropriate point in the meeting. Do not devote time to any more explanation of the process than necessary. Too much attention to process may cause some participants to feel their participation is being over-controlled when what you hope to do is get more balanced input from everyone.

Avoid situations likely to create defensive behavior.

When individuals state views that differ from the group, they can feel defensive and isolated. **1-2-All** and **PALPaR** are also effective in limiting defensive reactions and maintaining a productive discussion. **Forces Review** is another process that can help to structure a balanced exploration of differing viewpoints.

> **Multi-Voting**
> is a technique in which participants place colored, self-adhesive dots on various elements of some decision. Once all the dots are in place, the whole group reviews the pattern created and draws various conclusions.

Forces Review helps you engage everyone in identifying what is supporting or restraining forward progress on some effort. Once these forces are identified, you lead a discussion to identify what can be done to strengthen the supports or weaken the restraints. This process creates an open and constructive dialogue, one that is less focused on one or two difficult issues and engages everyone in identifying possible actions.

Forces Review is particularly helpful when you are trying to engage others in taking on some new initiative or supporting an organizational change. For example, I recently worked with a nonprofit organization to launch a new set of strategic initiatives. After a few months, they held a follow-up meeting to see how the change was progressing. Twenty people with a range of responsibilities were present. The Executive Director decided to use a **Forces Review** for this discussion.

Together they brainstormed all of the factors that could restrain progress with the new strategy. They also completed a brainstorm of all those factors that were supporting the success of this strategy. Using **Multi-Voting**, they identified the top three factors that were restraining progress and then the top three that were supporting progress. After reviewing the results with everyone, the leader divided the whole group in two. One half of the group was to focus on identifying ways to weaken the top three restraining factors. What could they do to make these less of a threat to the strategy's success? The other half of the group would work on ways to strengthen the top three supporting factors. These became creative, energized discussions. When both groups were done, the results were shared. The final step was to begin action planning to work with the ideas they had generated.

A second tool that I call **Future Focus** can help you create a productive discussion of some challenging situation while avoiding a group's tendency to blame someone or something for a past problem. For example, an agenda might list "yesterday's safety incident" for a management meeting after some accident. A more productive conversation is possible when the agenda item is more fully defined and focused on future performance: "What can we learn from yesterday's safety incident to improve workplace safety going forward?"

Finally, I recommend you avoid "straw votes" or other ways of making decisions based on a majority vote. Any form of up or down (binary) voting naturally produces "sides" and creates "winners" and "losers," none of which supports dialogue. Instead of binary voting, you can use **Multi-Voting** in which each person gets to place more than one "vote" (usually by placing colored, sticky dots or check marks) by various options. This creates a picture of preferences that the group can then interpret and build upon. I once served on a committee that met for 18 months to identify and recommend options for building a new school. Throughout that period, the committee never once took a traditional vote, since this would have split the committee into various sides of the issue. Instead, we used multi-voting to explore priorities and discuss preferences without creating more dissension and defensiveness.[xii]

> **Future Focus** is a simple process for engaging participants in defining the desired future solution rather than focusing on solving past problems.

Working with This Choice

Reflection. Consider how your meeting participants usually talk together. Does everyone get a chance to speak and be heard? Do some people speak less, maybe much less, than others? Do you know why?

You may have planned some structure to support better discussion given the ideas in chapter 3, but will this be enough? Should you anticipate the use of one or two other tools to address any challenges that may emerge this time?

Beginning to Make Changes. Choose one or two of the following tools that you feel would be most useful in some upcoming meeting.

- 1-2-All
- PALPaR

- **Go-Around**
- **Future Focus**
- **Multi-Voting**

Become familiar with the tool and how you would introduce it. Maybe you have a meeting coming up with a difficult discussion or larger group than usual. See if you can picture how you could build the tool's recommendations into the conduct of the meeting when you expect the conversation might become difficult. Try it out and then reflect on what worked for you and the group: Many times the success of the structures a tool creates lies in what didn't happen rather than what might have otherwise.

For Additional Support. More stories of the application of these tools can be found on my blog at **www.meetingforresults.com/ blog.**

Chapter 10

How You Manage Time

Good use of meeting time begins while planning the meeting (chapter 5). However, no matter how carefully you plan, there will be occasions when timing must be revised or reallocated during the course of the session. There are three specific steps you can take to manage time better as you lead discussions.

Share responsibility for timing.

Ask for a volunteer to take the responsibility of timekeeper (see **Four Responsibilities**). The most important benefit of this role comes when the timekeeper interrupts the discussion to give the group a "two minute warning" that time is about to run out. With everyone aware of the time, it may be possible to bring discussion to a close. If more time is needed, you can reallocate the time remaining in the agenda or ask the group if they are willing to extend the originally scheduled meeting time. See the tools **Time Renegotiation** and **Time Planning Tips** for more ideas.

Time Renegotiation is a practice for openly involving participants in the reallocation of available time when meeting demands change the original plan.

Provide clear guidelines for reports and discussion.

Many leaders lose control of time when an individual or group is reporting and various questions are being raised. Both the discussion and the intended timing can quickly get away from you. Instead, provide the following structure to manage the work to the time available:

- Specify the amount of time for a report to the whole group. This time can often be quite short if the reporting individual or group is asked to summarize conclusions. Five minutes or less is often enough.

- Hold questions and discussion until the end of any report. Explain up front that you'd like the group to hear the report(s) first before going into questions and discussions. See **Time Planning Tips** for more information.

Use visible note taking to track the discussion.

Finally, many meeting discussions lose time when the discussion begins to wander. A great way to help the group stay on track is to keep a real-time, visual record of key points and concerns raised. Individuals will see that their comments have been heard and the group as a whole can begin to monitor itself as it sees how various points connect to others. See **Visible Note Taking**.

Working with This Choice

Reflection. What are your typical challenges in managing meeting time? When the timing doesn't go as expected, was it unrealistic, and could you have anticipated this and had a simpler, more robust schedule? Did you lose control of time because of difficult and lengthy whole group discussions? Could you have planned a different structure for these discussions?

Beginning to Make Changes. One of the easiest tools to begin using is **Time Renegotiation**. Introducing this tool is simple. It also helps you share the responsibility of managing meeting time, so that your participants may begin to take more control of their own actions.

Chapter 11

How You Work with Any Conflict

Most approaches to managing difficult conversations emphasize adopting behaviors such as asking open ended questions, suspending judgment, and so on. By now you know that I'm going to recommend an approach that is more structural than behavioral. You need something you can use on the spot to create a structure for a respectful exchange, avoid defensive behaviors, and limit the chance of individuals becoming polarized on some issue. There are three ways you can work with conflict, either because you anticipate that it may arise, or to respond in the moment.

Provide for small group sharing of views before the whole group discussion.

One way to deal with (anticipated) conflict is to provide opportunities for small group conversation *before* whole group discussion. If you think there is likely to be a range of reactions to some proposal, plan for sharing those reactions in small groups first. Exchanging views in a small group enables individuals to express their opinions in a setting where they may receive some feedback and can modify or incorporate their views with others. Tools such as **1-2-All**, **PALPaR**, and **Three Reaction Questions** can help you do this. **Three Reaction Questions** focuses on eliciting positive reactions first, which makes sure that what is appreciated does not get overwhelmed by more negative concerns.

Provide for a balanced review.

Any conflict frequently focuses on a few difficult areas. Switching the focus of the discussion to a more balanced perspective can help the group move forward. One way to do this is by conducting a **Forces Review**. This tool helps you structure a balanced review of a range of factors affecting the situation. It creates a productive exchange of views and keeps everyone engaged in the work of the meeting. See the example of its use in chapter 9.

A **Go-Around** can be helpful to air a range of views without emphasizing sides. It can be introduced in the moment when the group is getting stuck. As you introduce this process, be careful that you don't imply that you are trying to confirm where the majority stand on the issue or otherwise use the weight of group opinion to "silence" some dissenting view. Simply explain that you'd like to hear a brief comment from each participant on where they stand relative to the issue. It can help to note that this is an opportunity for each person to express his/her view, but not to argue against someone else's view.

Focus on future action as opposed to past problems.

Finally, you can focus the discussion on desires for the future and avoid rehashing past problems. People find it easier to align around future plans than they do resolving past concerns. Focusing on the past can make some people feel defensive around any suspected attempt to assign guilt or innocence. See **Future Focus** in the *Tool Chest* for more information.

Working with This Choice

Reflection. What types of conflict typically arise in your meetings? Is it more likely to be generated by certain people or issues? Are there differing views that people don't feel comfortable discussing in your meetings?

Beginning to Make Changes. If some conflict seems likely, select an approach that you feel comfortable using and plan when you might use it. **1-2-All**, **Forces Review**, **PALPaR**, and **Three Reaction Questions** are easiest to introduce with a little forethought. A **Go-Around** can be introduced on the spot when needed.

PART III:

Two Final Choices for Achieving Results from Your Meeting

Two final choices can help you create a structure to support achieving results from your meeting. These choices are particularly important when your intended outcomes involve some group decision and follow-up actions. The two choices are:

1) How you build decisions.

2) How you follow up.

You should consider these choices as you first plan the meeting, but you will implement them near the end of your meeting and in subsequent follow-up activities.

Chapter 12

How You Build Decisions

Decisions can be built (rather than "made") in ways that engage and align people around conclusions. This means developing decisions through a process that respects and incorporates various views. Such an approach increases engagement and the likelihood of commitment to the overall decision, even where disagreement remains on some points.

There are a variety of actions you can take to structure how you build decisions with your group. Below are six different actions from which you can choose in approaching a given situation.

Be clear about how you expect to reach a decision with your group.

You should choose and communicate your intended means of reaching a decision with your group (one of the **Five Cs**) as you first introduce the decision to be made. Then act consistently with your choice. Avoid "putting your finger on the scale" by leading the discussion in a way that emphasizes your own preferences. For example, don't say something like, "Does anyone see a problem with proceeding on…," or "Unless I hear an objection, I assume we all agree on this." Instead, choose the approach that accurately reflects how you want to work with the group on this decision, describe this approach, and act accordingly. See **Five Cs** in the *Tool Chest* for more on these choices and their relative strengths and weaknesses.

Five Cs is a tool for reviewing and selecting among the ways of making a decision with a group: **C**onsensus, **C**onsent, **C**ompromise, **C**ounting (votes), and **C**onsulting.

Organize ideas and options in ways that allow all to explore their relationships.

Create a visual means of organizing key components in the decision. Use sticky notes and various graphic devices to display the components so that participants can see different relationships, move items around and otherwise "play" with the concepts. (See **Affinity Grouping** for help with this).

Set up a structure for your discussion that respects all points of view.

Use a process that shows you want to hear all views, including opposing ones. This can be as simple as making sure all can speak and be heard without creating a debate. By being open to hearing different views, you may find areas of agreement within the disagreements, and avoid creating factions or otherwise isolating people. (See **Consensus Guidelines**, **Forces Review**, **Go-Around**, and **PALPaR** for ways to do this.)

Affinity Grouping is a process for organizing diverse ideas to help a group recognize similarities and differences among suggestions.

Provide a visual record of the discussion.

Visible Note Taking, **Affinity Grouping**, and **Multi-Voting** are all helpful here. **Visible Note Taking** helps everyone see the progress of the discussion. **Affinity Grouping** and **Multi-Voting** provide feedback to everyone on how the group's views are distributed. This can help to identify priorities and suggest interrelationships. Note, I do not recommend taking an "up or down" vote, unless you actually chose voting (the fourth "C" for "counting") as the way you want to achieve a decision. If you need to take a vote for the record, arrive at the group decision first and then take the vote. See **Five Cs** and **Multi-Voting** in the *Tool Chest* for more information. The first "blueprint" for a problem-solving meeting in chapter 14 contains an example of **Multi-Voting** in use.

Act on areas of agreement and respect, but don't focus on areas of disagreement.

Highlight areas of agreement and recognize but don't dwell on areas of disagreement. This reverses the usual use of time and energy in discussions where almost all the attention is given to the difficult areas. By focusing on areas of agreement you can use this positive energy to move forward with the group. By recognizing the areas of disagreement, you respect these as areas that deserve more attention in the future. You want the group to make the decision it can for now and to begin taking action. See **80/20 Principle** in the *Tool Chest* for more on this.

Here's an example of how focusing on areas of agreement works. I once facilitated a process improvement effort in a manufacturing plant. A cross-section of the whole plant met together for more than a day to decide on their vision and action plans for improvement. When it finally came down to deciding on specific areas for improvement, one idea generated a wide range of opinions. It involved creating a larger warehouse. Some participants felt that more warehouse space was needed in order to organize the production areas. Others felt that improvements in the plant's processes would make more warehouse space unnecessary. I had already introduced the **80/20 Principle**, and I reminded them of it when they couldn't agree. They put increased warehouse space on a list of items to revisit again in a few months once work had begun on the improvements that all supported. Then they began to work on the items they all supported. When the group met again to review their progress later in the year, they realized they no longer needed more warehouse space and instead were ready to convert some of the original warehouse space for use in a new production line.[xiii]

Don't put yourself in the middle of some disagreement unless the final decision was always intended to be yours alone.

Instead, use the wisdom in the group. If the group's discussion gets stuck, ask, *"What do you want to do?"* Allow the group to participate in deciding how to proceed. Is there some first step that all can agree on? If you have built the basis for respectful discussion throughout the meeting, then the group should have some shared ownership for a successful outcome and want to define the way forward.

The **80/20 Principle** refers to a tendency of many groups to focus on areas of disagreement while ignoring the areas of agreement. You can use it as a "ground rule" to help a group focus on the 80% they agree on to begin making progress and avoid getting stuck in their disagreements.

Working with This Choice

Reflection. What types of decisions do you typically address in your meetings? Are any decisions usually well supported by the group? Do you have real commitment or just compliance with those decisions? Or do some decisions tend to fall apart afterwards? Do you find yourself making more unilateral decisions because it seems too hard to work with the group?

Beginning to Make Changes. The most important change you may need to make is to be clearer about how you expect to involve the group in any decision. Choose and communicate which of the **Five Cs** you wish to use before your next discussion. You can do this without making a big point of it, but just be clear about your expectations.

One of the more useful tools for building group alignment around some decision is **Forces Review**. This tool supports a balanced exploration of forces working for or against some plan or decision. You can use it to test a decision before it is made or to plan for implementation of a decision once it has been reached. It also enables you to identify a balanced set of action items to put the decision into practice. Chapter 9 includes a story of **Forces Review** in use. And the "blueprint" for the second problem-solving meeting in chapter 14 outlines an application of **Forces Review** in detail.

For more about the advantages of acknowledging but not "working" areas of disagreement see Weisbord and Janoff (2010, 87).

Chapter 13

How You Follow Up

Good follow up is critical for implementing many meeting outcomes. Done well it helps individuals and organizations learn from past actions and achieve better results. Such follow up requires a structure that enables participants to reflect on progress in a balanced and timely way. Any practice that causes people to feel their actions are being evaluated will create defensiveness and less commitment to keep working on the original plans.

There are three actions you can take to create the structure for a productive follow-up session:

Have the individual(s) responsible for any follow-up action present when the action is initially planned.

Action plans are a common and valuable practice in many meetings. Sometimes, however, actions are defined and assigned to people not present. Developing action plans with the involvement of individuals directly responsible is essential to ensure ownership of next steps. Therefore, it pays to give careful consideration to who gets invited to your meetings. See chapter 2 for more information.

Use a balanced set of "follow-up" questions to create a productive review of progress.

Many follow-up discussions focus on the reasons that initial plans have not been completed as intended. Little attention is given to recognizing the progress made or what can be learned from successes and failures thus far. A more productive review can be conducted by using **Three Follow-Up Questions** as the framework for reporting on progress:

1) What has been accomplished as planned?

2) What hasn't been accomplished as planned?

3) What are we learning about making progress in this area from our answers to questions 1 and 2?[xiv]

The answers to these three questions make any follow-up conversation an opportunity to reflect on past actions and plan to move forward. The answer to the first question is often revealing and energizing. Sometimes, people forget what they have accomplished and focus only on actions that have been hard to complete, since that is where they feel some tension. Addressing these first two questions in this order creates a more positive context for the follow-up review. Finally, the third question turns this review of past actions into proactive problem solving and planning. See **Three Follow-Up Questions** for more information.

Note: Replies to each of the three questions for follow up is best done on a general level. If some detailed information on progress is needed, it can help to address the questions first and then hear the detail. If you do this the other way around, some of the learning about leading effective actions may get lost.

Make sure a follow-up review occurs within 30-45 days of the original meeting.

Many follow-up conversations are too late to be effective. We may have planned a follow-up conversation for some convenient time on the organization's calendar (e.g., the next quarterly team meeting). Waiting this long, however, usually creates difficulties. Once several months have passed since we committed to some actions, we forget initial accomplishments. We have mentally checked them off as done. They are no longer something we think about. Instead we are more aware of what has *not* been done and may focus on reasons that original plans were unrealistic to relieve the stress of failing to make progress. As a result, it becomes more likely that the intentions of the initial action planning will be lost.

I have worked on follow-up activities with dozens of teams in different organizations. Over and over again, I have found that a period of four to six weeks is about the *maximum* length of time to wait to hold a productive review of accomplishments. Any longer than this and people have forgotten initial progress and instead have "learned" many good reasons for not completing the original plans.

Working with This Choice

Reflection. What is your personal experience of follow up on planned actions? For example, do you make "to do" lists for the weekend? If so, what do you pay most attention to when the weekend ends—those items you accomplished or the ones you never completed? I know I tend to overlook, even forget, my accomplishments and focus instead on the incomplete items. This is why the **Three Follow-Up Questions** can be so helpful.

Beginning to Make Changes. This choice is one of the easiest to implement in most situations…as long as your meeting resulted in a clear set of action items. Simply schedule a meeting a few weeks later and use the **Three Follow-Up Questions**. If you have small groups working on different actions, have them meet for a few minutes to develop their replies to the questions.

Part IV

Can You See Me Now? Structuring Effective Virtual Meetings

It was late in the day. Mary had scheduled this time for a virtual meeting to accommodate participant schedules across three time zones. She had sent out a general agenda well in advance with the meeting invitation. Several decisions needed to be made, and she hoped all would be present for this important discussion.

While all had accepted the meeting "invite," only five of the eight participants were present as the meeting began. One participant sent a text message to say he was running late. Mary hadn't heard from the others, so she began anyway. After five minutes, the discussion was interrupted as someone joined. Mary stopped, welcomed the latecomer and explained where they were in the discussion. The meeting proceeded until another person joined a few minutes later. Mary stopped again to bring this person up to speed. Shortly thereafter, this happened a third time.

It was almost 15 minutes into the scheduled time for the call when Mary was able to continue without interruption. By now the discussion on the first agenda item was running long. Also, one person seemed confused about the progress of the discussion. He had been the last to arrive and hadn't heard some of the earlier discussion.

Eventually the group seemed to arrive at a decision. Mary began to wrap up. *"I think we've heard from everyone and we all seem to generally support this idea, so I suggest we move on."* But then, a voice broke in, *"Sorry, I tried to say something but forgot that I was on mute. I have a serious concern with adopting this approach. I'd like to talk about it…"* This reopened the discussion, which ran on

Nancy Settle-Murphy provided many ideas and suggestions for this chapter. For more information, see her book *Leading Effective Virtual Teams* (2013) or see her tips and newsletter at **www. guidedinsights.com**.

for another several minutes. Finally, Mary summarized what she thought was the overall conclusion and moved to the next item on the agenda.

The meeting was now running well behind schedule with just 15 minutes remaining. As Mary went on to the next agenda item, one participant interrupted to apologize for having to leave the call early and hung up. The remaining participants struggled to accomplish what they could with the time left. Some items would have to be addressed off-line or in the next meeting. Afterwards, Mary felt frustrated by her inability to achieve all she had planned.

Does Mary's situation sound familiar? Virtual meetings pose some common challenges not always present in typical face-to-face meetings. For various reasons, virtual meeting participants are more likely to exhibit certain (dysfunctional) behaviors, such as showing up late, leaving early, being unprepared, multi-tasking, remaining silent, talking over others, or listening in without announcing their presence. Perhaps this problematic behavior happens because people can't be seen, or because a "virtual" meeting is viewed as somehow less legitimate than a face-to-face meeting. Whatever the reason, virtual meeting leaders face many unique challenges that call for special techniques.

Note: Tools adapted for virtual meetings have "**VM**" as a superscript at the end of their names to distinguish them from similar tools for face-to-face meetings (e.g., **Go-Around^{VM}**).

To bring some order to your virtual meetings, you need to plan and implement a structure that reflects these challenges. Although many of us do prepare for virtual meetings, much of this preparation may be devoted to making sure we have the technology working. While technology is important, there are other aspects of a virtual meeting you need to address if it is to be effective.

This chapter reviews how the 12 choices for structuring effective meetings apply to virtual ones along with various tools that can help you implement your choices.

At the end of this chapter, I will return to Mary's experience to explain how she resolved her challenges.

Planning Choices for Virtual Meetings

How You Define the Work of the Meeting

For virtual discussions, it is particularly important to be clear, up front, about the purpose of any specific discussion items. A virtual meeting participant who doesn't understand the purpose is likely to disengage or to disrupt the discussion with basic questions. Fulfilling the criteria of the **FATT** tool acronym (**F**ocused, **A**ctionable, **T**imely and **T**imed) for each agenda item is *even more important*. Be explicit in your meeting notification, and invite people to respond in advance if they have other ideas or questions.

Who Gets Invited

Careful selection of participants can ensure that the relevant perspectives are present for the discussion. Virtual meetings make it easier to have a few additional people join the discussion for just the topics of relevance to them. However, you need to consider how well people know each other. Some individuals can be reluctant to share their thoughts in the presence of strangers they do not even see. A **Go-Around**VM as you begin can welcome all into the "room." You should also consider which people have to participate in a real-time discussion, as opposed to participating in another way at another time. Holding in-depth discussions becomes difficult with more than six or seven people.

How You Design the Discussion

In virtual sessions, it is easy for participants to withhold comments or not to be fully engaged in the work. "Hybrid" meetings in which some participants are face-to-face and others participate from remote locations make it even harder to engage everyone equally.

There are three opportunities to prepare a better structure for engaging everyone in an effective discussion.

Before the meeting:

- Send out a list of meeting participant names and locations. Enclose pictures of participants. Better yet, create a slide that shows everyone around a table, complete with photos and names. Ask people to have this handy for the actual meeting. Set up a time for those individuals who are new to the group to meet others in brief one-to-one calls prior to the meeting.

- Identify individuals to take on specific roles in conducting the meeting. See **Five Responsibilities**VM for more on this. Doing this in advance of the meeting enables your "volunteers" to come prepared for their roles as time-keeper, recorder, and so on.

As the meeting begins:

- Plan to have each participant introduce him/herself in a brief **Go-Around**VM. This can also be done in a separate virtual conference call prior to the meeting, especially if there are more than eight participants on the call.

Go-AroundVM gives each person a brief turn to speak to the topic, without interruption, while everyone listens. For a virtual meeting, it is usually important to do a **Go-Around**VM at frequent points throughout a discussion to ensure that anyone who might want to make a comment has an opportunity to be heard.

Five ResponsibilitiesVM describes the five different responsibilities that need to be fulfilled to varying degrees for an effective virtual meeting. It includes an additional role of Technology Minder.

During the meeting:

- Plan to address participants by name on a regular basis to give everyone a chance to be heard and keep all engaged. Use **Go-Around**VM as necessary. Having a copy of your team member's pictures handy can help you track participation and note important comments.

- Presentations should be given a set, limited time. The **PIP** presentation guidelines are particularly critical to virtual meetings where timelines are usually tight and the presenter gets little non-verbal feedback while speaking. Try to limit presentation time to no more than five minutes without some kind of interaction.

If you have a big group (more than eight), it is a challenge to keep all engaged. Using small group discussion (e.g., **1-2-All**) may be difficult or impossible depending on your technology. Fortunately, you still have ways to structure an effective virtual discussion with some advance planning. Here's how:

- **Prework and asynchronous participation.** There are various ways to engage participants in sharing ideas outside the real-time meeting. On-line conference areas and community forums, shared comments on documents, and pre-meeting calls between participants are all options to consider.

- **Polls and other means of sharing the work of the meeting.** Various techniques for polling participant views are available depending on your technology. You can plan to do this much as you would **Multi-Voting** in a face-to-face meeting. As always, be careful using any binary, yes/no voting as that can polarize the group.

- **Information management.** Plan to share copies of key documents and presentations in advance, to minimize the time devoted to presenting this information in the meeting. Let people know why you are sending the material ahead of time, and make it clear why reviewing this content will be important. All documents should be explicitly labeled for ease of reference. If you are asking people to review a lot of content (e.g. requiring more than a half-hour's worth of preparation), let them know which sections are most crucial for them to review, and why.

How You Intend to Reach Decisions

Virtual meetings are not very different from face-to-face meetings in how you reach decisions with a group, but you have to make a few adjustments.

- It still pays to be clear about how a decision is to be reached (see the **Five Cs**).

- **PALPaR** can be used without modification for virtual meetings, as it provides a structure for a decision where the leader will be the final decider based on the group's input.

- Tools like **Affinity Grouping** or **Multi-Voting** may be used, with adjustments, depending on the capabilities of the virtual meeting technology in use.

- Many software applications enable you to share a virtual "white board" or flip chart with a group so you can record ideas and move them around as if you were working in one room together.

- Some virtual meeting platforms also allow for quick and easy polling so you can learn how all are thinking about some point. Some audio-conferencing tools allow quick polling as well.

- If this virtual meeting is to be conducted as an audio-only conference call, you can still use a **Go-Around**VM to support decision making.

How You Plan to "Spend" Meeting Time

Virtual meetings pose distinctive timing challenges. First, they need to be kept short. Ninety minutes is about as long as you can expect to keep participants engaged. Sixty minutes or less may be more practical. And since participants often schedule other appointments right up to the time of a virtual session, you can improve participation by not scheduling your meeting to begin or end right on the hour or half-hour.

Second, you need to give extra attention to creating a realistic design for how the time will be allocated. Do not try to cram too many items into one meeting and risk running out of time; you may not be able to ask people to stay on the call longer than planned. To improve your timing, see **Time Planning Tips**VM and then create a realistic and detailed **STARS** agenda.

Third, virtual meetings create particular challenges for managing late arrivals. I expect you have been in virtual meetings that go through multiple restarts and introductions as participants arrive to the meeting after the discussion has begun. This problem is not so bad in a face-to-face meeting, as participants can see who is arriving. No one has to stop the flow of discussion to ask *"Who just joined?"*

Time Planning TipsVM provides recommendations for structuring a realistic use of time in a virtual meeting, as such sessions need to be kept relatively short (60-90 minutes or less) to keep people engaged and end on time.

While you may not be able to control late arrivals, you can take several steps to make them less likely and less disruptive when they do occur.

- Set up any necessary technology to be fully operational for anyone to call in approximately ten minutes before the meeting is scheduled to begin. When you announce the meeting, ask participants to join the meeting a few minutes early to make sure the technology is working.

- Announce and follow your intent to start on time.

- Begin the meeting with a **Go-Around**[VM] to enable everyone to check in and get engaged. Doing this has a second benefit: A brief round of introductions will take a few minutes and gives you a chance to include any late arrivals. In my experience, a check-in is almost never a waste of meeting time.

- If someone arrives still later, you can stop for a moment and note briefly where you are on the agenda, but then keep going with your meeting. Don't backtrack or summarize what has already been discussed as this "rewards" the late individual and bores everyone else.

How You Arrange the Virtual Meeting Space

The physical environment of virtual meetings "permits" distractions, inattention, and parallel processing. However, a virtual meeting held under effective physical conditions can support better focus, more engagement and productive use of time by all present.

Consider the following physical variables as you plan your meeting:

- **Participant location.** Are all participants separate from each other, or are some together in one room? A hybrid meeting puts those who are remote at a disadvantage compared to those meeting together in one location. You should take additional steps to ensure a hybrid meeting will engage everyone. See **Hybrid Meeting Checklist**[VM] for more on this.

- **Virtual meeting technology.** Visual support for most meetings is very helpful if not essential. The better the visual support, not just for sharing documents but for seeing other participants, the more engaging your meeting is likely to be. Use the best technology you can, but make sure everyone can use it. You don't want to create two "classes" of participants—those who can see what's going on and those who can't.

Hybrid Meeting Checklist[VM] is a set of guidelines for conducting effective discussions when some participants are meeting face-to-face while one or more others are "virtual participants" using audio conferencing or other technology.

- **"Sound check."** Check that you and everyone else can use the technology as intended in advance of the meeting. You will also need to make sure everyone has the instructions for joining. People often fail to have the right number or conference link when needed, or haven't downloaded the latest revision of a given virtual meeting software application.

- **Audio.** Ensure good quality audio by using "land lines" and/or headsets. Avoid speakerphones or microphones built into computers.

- **Visuals.** Share pictures of everyone attending on one page or screen. Pictures of participants, even static clippings, help to connect a voice with a face and can remind you who has/hasn't spoken. During the meeting, plan to maintain visible notes in real time to help everyone see the progress of discussions. See **Visible Note Taking**VM for more information.

For more on these and other arrangements for effective virtual meeting space see **Meeting "Room" Checklist**VM.

Using the Results of This Planning to Create the Agenda for Your Virtual Meeting

A well-defined **STARS** agenda has the same benefits for leading virtual meetings as it does for face-to-face ones—or even more. This is partly because nonverbal feedback during the meeting is limited if present at all, so a carefully developed agenda helps everyone stay "on the same page." For example, a well-defined agenda is needed to help all understand both the purpose of and the time available for a particular discussion. Time allocation can be particularly critical—it must be adequate for the task and expected participation, but it also needs to be kept as short and focused as possible to maintain engagement. Also, try to avoid including items such as "updates" that may be effectively communicated in another manner. For more information, see **STARS** in the *Tool Chest* and examples of **STARS** agendas in chapters 7 and 14.

Conducting Choices for Virtual Meetings

How You Share Responsibility

Leading a virtual meeting can require more multitasking than a face-to-face meeting. Instead of assuming all the responsibilities as the leader, divide up the roles across meeting participants. See **Five Responsibilities**VM. Identify who will take on these responsibilities before the meeting begins so that the volunteers know how to use any necessary technology.

Visible Note TakingVM supports the group's memory of what it has discussed and how its decisions are evolving. It shows each participant that his or her comments were heard and helps all keep track of the progress of discussions.

Meeting "Room" ChecklistVM provides a set of requirements for an effective virtual meeting environment, one that is more likely to support and maintain participant engagement.

How You Support Productive Conversations

The benefits and requirements of good dialogue don't change because you are in a virtual setting. Here it is even more important that all participants get to share their thinking and listen to each other respectfully. You can make good use of **Go-Around**[VM] and **Three Reaction Questions**. **Go-Around**[VM] is particularly important to balance air time, to keep all engaged, and to make up for the lack of nonverbal feedback on some point. You should plan to use it throughout the meeting whenever it is important to get everyone's input.

How You Manage Time

In spite of the best-made plans, the time required for some parts of a meeting are likely to change. Having a timekeeper can help, as can the tool, **Time Renegotiation**.

How You Work With Any Conflict

A virtual meeting creates some challenging conditions for those holding dissenting views. Someone who speaks out against some point can be taking more risk since s/he may get less verbal or nonverbal feedback. **Go-Around**[VM] can again be helpful here—if it is set up so as not to sound like an up-or-down "vote." Instead, ask people to reply where they are right now on the issue at hand. Other tools introduced for face-to-face meetings work fine too, like **Future Focus** and **Three Reaction Questions**. The technique I call **Forces Review** can be used if your technology supports some level of real-time, visible note taking. Depending on your virtual meeting technology, you may also be able to do some form of **Multi-Voting** to quickly portray the range of views on some question.

Achieving Results in Virtual Meetings

How You Build Decisions

You can use most of the approaches of a face-to-face meeting to arrive at a decision in a virtual meeting. First, choose how you want to arrive at a decision using the **Five Cs**, and make sure the group understands the choice. However, you may need to consider the limits of your virtual meeting technology as you choose your decision-making approach. Highly visual and interactive tools like **Affinity Grouping** and **Multi-Voting** may be practical or not, depending on your technology. But, no matter what your technology, you still can use **Go-Around**[VM], **PALPaR**, and **Three Reaction Questions**.

How You Follow Up

Your choices and tools here remain the same as they are with a face-to-face meeting.

Putting It All Together: Something More about Mary

Let's return to Mary's virtual meetings. Mary had called me for help shortly after the meeting I described earlier. As she explained her frustrating experience, I recommended various steps she could take to structure her meetings to manage these challenges. She later called back to describe what she did next and what happened.

Planning the Meeting

Her first decision was to schedule the next meeting to last for 50 minutes rather than an hour. She would ask for everyone's full participation for that whole period, given that they would end early so participants could make any subsequent appointment. She clarified the intended outcomes of all agenda items and reviewed them with several participants, to make sure there was enough time for the expected discussion. She wanted the purpose of discussions to be clear with a realistic amount of time specified.

As she completed the agenda, she began to think about how she would lead the discussion. To balance participation and build clearer decisions, she decided to conduct a **Go-Around**^{VM} several times—first at the beginning to hear from everyone as they arrived, and later as they reached key closure on several agenda items. Finally, she added thumbnail pictures of each participant to help all remember who would be speaking during the call.

Mary then contacted two participants, Sue and Frank, to support her in running the meeting. She asked Sue to be the timekeeper and explained that she should give the group a "time check" when there were three minutes remaining on any particular agenda item. Mary asked Frank to take notes where all could see them as the discussion proceeded, using a shared, online file. She asked him to set up the document and become familiar with how it worked before the meeting. When Mary sent out the agenda and calling instructions, she included the link to the document so everyone could see Frank's ongoing notes during the meeting. She also made sure that Sue and Frank could communicate directly with her using instant messaging if they had a question about their roles during the meeting.

Conducting the Meeting

All but one of the participants were present at the start of the meeting. Mary began the **Go-Around**[VM] by asking each person to note any question s/he had when reviewing the agenda, and made sure that Frank captured the responses. Mary spoke first to break the ice and to model the kind of response she was looking for, and then ended by asking *"who's next?"* As different individuals spoke, Mary checked her group photo to make sure that no one was missed. About halfway through the check-in, one last person arrived. Mary welcomed her and explained where they were in the agenda.

Mary then introduced the first main agenda item. She explained that she had asked Sue to keep track of the time and Frank to outline the progress of their discussion online where all could see the document. The discussion proceeded. Twenty minutes had been allocated.

Sue notified the group shortly before the allotted time was over. Mary asked, *"Are you ready to make a decision or do we need more time?"* Several people said they were ready and so Mary explained she wanted to **Go-Around**[VM] again to hear from each person in turn without any discussion until all had spoken. She asked, *"Could you each briefly explain your support or note any remaining questions or reservations?"* Frank tracked the comments as they were made and Mary spoke last.

When all had spoken, there were two questions to be resolved. Mary asked, *"Should we spend another five minutes resolving these questions now, or take these items offline and go ahead with the decision as it stands for now?"* Two individuals volunteered to resolve the remaining questions offline. Mary then checked with those who had raised the questions, *"Can we proceed with this plan assuming these questions will be resolved?"* They agreed, and Mary moved to the next agenda item.

Twenty minutes remained in the meeting. The discussion of this item proceeded quickly. All seemed ready to move to a decision just as Sue gave the three-minute warning. Mary conducted another **Go-Around**[VM] to conclude the decision making.

As the meeting ended, Mary reviewed the action items, which Frank had recorded for all to see, and thanked Sue and Frank for their help with the meeting. Several participants expressed their appreciation for a productive session.

When Mary spoke to me, she was feeling much better about her ability to get work done in a virtual meeting. But, she asked, would the next meeting go as well? I explained that the continued success of these meetings would depend on beginning and ending on time with all contributing to a respectful discussion. These were the precedents she had set and, as long as she maintained them, she could expect more effective participation.

Tools to Use in Implementing Your Virtual Meeting Choices

The table on the following page presents the choices and supporting tools relevant for virtual meetings. Some tools remain the same as for face-to-face meetings, but you will also note some additional tools designed or modified for virtual meetings. These tools have "**VM**" as a superscript at the end of their name. New tools are underlined in the table.

Six Choices in Planning	Supporting Tools
1 How you define the work of the meeting.	FATT
2 Who gets invited.	ARE IN Diagonal Slice
3 How you design the discussion.	Go-Around^{VM} PALPaR PIP Hybrid Meeting Checklist^{VM}
4 How you intend to reach decisions.	Five Cs Consensus Guidelines
5 How you plan to "spend" meeting time.	Time Planning Tips^{VM}
6 How you arrange the meeting space.	Meeting "Room" Checklist^{VM} Hybrid Meeting Checklist^{VM}
All of which lead to an agenda based on planning choices.	**STARS** agenda

Planning Choices^{VM}

Conducting ChoicesVM

Four Choices While Conducting	Supporting Tools
1 How you share responsibility.	**Five Responsibilities**VM **Visible Note Taking**VM
2 How you support productive conversations.	**Go-Around**VM **PALPaR** **Three Reaction Questions**
3 How you manage time.	**Time Renegotiation**
4 How you work with any conflict.	**Forces Review** **Future Focus** **PALPaR** **Go-Around**VM

Achieving Results ChoicesVM

Two Choices for Achieving Results	Supporting Tools
1 How you build decisions.	**Go-Around**VM **PALPaR** **80/20 Principle**
2 How you follow up.	**Follow-Up Timing** **Three Follow-Up Questions**

Part V

Not the Usual 12-Step Program: The Path to Changing Your Meetings

The 12 structural choices are not intended to be a fixed process. While it helps to start with planning choices, you can start almost anywhere and improve some aspects of your next meeting's structure.

You may want to begin improving your meetings by making a few changes and observing your results. You can focus on the choices and tools that seem easiest to adopt in your situation. Here are a few places where you might want to begin.

How You Define the Work of the Meeting

One of the easiest ways to help a group have a productive meeting is to make sure any discussion task is clear and relevant to everyone. **FATT** reminds you to create a **Focused, Actionable, Timely,** and **Timed** description of each piece of work to be done. You should see an improvement in the efficiency and effectiveness of discussions when you clearly define the intended purpose or outcome of any given point on the agenda.

How You Design the Discussion

With groups larger than eight, it can be difficult to keep everyone engaged and contributing. **1-2-All** enables you to give participants an opportunity to organize and share their thoughts while managing the discussion in a limited amount of time.

How You Arrange the Meeting Space

Use the **Meeting Room Checklist** or **Meeting "Room" Checklist**[VM] (for virtual meetings) to create the best physical environment for your meeting.

How You Share Responsibility in Conducting the Meeting

Many of us try to do it all, from leading discussions to taking notes and managing time. **Four Responsibilities** and **Five Responsibilities**[VM] help you share roles for running a successful meeting. This not only makes your job easier, but also builds a sense of mutual ownership for a well-run meeting.

How You Support Productive Conversations

Try using **Three Reaction Questions** after some proposal has been introduced to the group. Afterward, notice how much more balanced the group's reactions were than they might have been.

If you are reading this shortly before your next meeting, you may want to implement one or two changes right away. Refer to the *Tool Chest* to find directions for the tools you want to use.

You also may want to look at the examples and stories in Part VI to see how others have adapted the choices and tools to fit various meeting situations. There you will find recommendations of choices or tools to adopt in typical meeting situations. If you are facing a specific challenge, you may want to review chapter 16. That chapter highlights a few choices and tools that may be helpful when you have little time to plan a better structure, as well as in "emergencies" when a discussion is going nowhere.

Finally, I recommend that you find someone to be a partner as you begin to make changes. Your partner can provide some insights into how you used some tool based on their observations. This person will understand what you are trying to change, and can give you some perspective and feedback on how you are doing.

Using the Tools: Some Things Are Best Left Unsaid

I find it is often easier if you don't explain the whole process of some tool you are using. *Just use it*. People appreciate clear leadership of a discussion as long as they don't feel manipulated, and some people may resist anything they feel is too much "process."

Participants will follow some simple, logical request, even if it is a little different from the usual practice. If I get a direct question about some change, I just answer it. For example, if someone asks why I have asked everyone to take different seats than usual, I might say that this is simply to give us all the possibility of different interactions around the table. If you are referring to notes on a tool in the meeting and get a question, explain that you are following suggestions to help you run the meeting effectively, but don't go into a detailed explanation. The tools are all clear and logical enough that there should be little to question.

The only exception to the recommendation to "just do it" is when a particular tool involves a multi-step process and people have to understand how the process works in order to participate effectively. **PALPaR** is the best example of this as it requires some explanation of how the feedback will be listened to but responded to at some later time (even if this is only after a brief break). **Forces Review** needs some explanation of process, but it can be done just one step at a time. With any tool, don't go into any more detail than necessary to take the next step with your group, or you may find yourself defending the process rather than doing the work of the meeting.

What Is the Current State of Your Meetings?

One place to start improving your meetings is by understanding how well they work (or don't) for you and your organization today. This can give you insights into specific opportunities for initial improvements.

The following pages present a form for reviewing your local meeting culture. Working from your own responses, you can focus on the accompanying notes and suggestions to make improvements. You may also want to give the survey to others to complete and use as the basis for a group discussion about changing local practices. You can download a copy at **www.MeetingforResults.com**.

Whatever you do, begin making changes and observe what happens. I know even one or two structural changes can make a difference in the productivity of meetings.

Meeting Culture Survey

How frequently do you lead or participate in meetings that exhibit the characteristics listed below? Evaluate your experience of meetings by rating each characteristic using the scale below. Add up your ratings and write the total in the box at the bottom. Then, turn the page to interpret your score.

1	2	3	4	5
Almost never	Seldom	Sometimes	Often	Almost always

The meetings I run or attend ...

a) _____ Have a well-defined agenda sent out in advance.

b) _____ Have a clear purpose or outcome for each main discussion item on the agenda.

c) _____ Include the "right" participants for the discussion, sometimes adding new participants with a range of perspectives and responsibilities relative to the subject.

d) _____ Begin and end on time with everyone present.

e) _____ Give all a chance to speak with no one person dominating.

f) _____ Limit the time spent on presentations and devote most of the time to discussion. Any necessary background information is sent out in advance.

g) _____ Are held in a comfortable space where all can see and hear each other equally well. Or they are held in an effective virtual setting.

h) _____ Maintain a focused, respectful discussion.

i) _____ Have a clearly identified way to reach decisions–as a group or by the leader.

j) _____ Have participants share responsibilities for note taking and keeping track of time.

k) _____ Readjust time for various agenda items to manage the work of the meeting to the overall time available.

l) _____ Are followed by clear, useful notes documenting any discussions or decisions.

m) _____ Result in action items with effective follow up.

Total score:

Interpreting Your Score

If your total score is between:

52 - 65	**Congratulations! You should be having many highly effective meetings.** If there is any one area where you gave yourself a low score, you may want to see what you can do to improve in that area.
39 - 51	**You should be having fairly effective meetings, but you could be failing to get the real engagement and results you want.** Identify one or two areas for improvement first, and see the choices and tools in this book for ideas on how to improve. Once you feel confident with your meeting performance in these areas, move on to others. You do not have to improve all areas at once. Note: items a, b, e, and j are usually the most visible, immediate areas for improvement. If you scored poorly in one of these areas, these could be a good place to begin. Better advance planning (item a) makes such improvement possible. Items d and k support each other. See **Time Planning Tips** or **Time Planning Tips**^{VM} for ideas on meeting time management.
26 - 38	**You are having difficult meetings!** In all likelihood they are not helping you to lead effectively. Pick one or two items from the list that you feel ready to improve and begin. Items a, b, d, e, and j are the most visible, immediate areas for improvement. If you scored poorly in one or more of these areas, you may want to begin making changes here. Items d and k support each other. After you have made progress in your first one or two areas, keep working on additional areas. Note: the last area for attention is item c. If you have the choice, you only want to invite additional participants when you feel confident in your ability to hold effective meetings with your usual, presumably smaller, group.
13 - 25	**Yikes!** You are probably being too hard on yourself. For now, pick one or two items from the list that you feel ready to improve. Items a, b, d, e, j, and k are likely to be the most visible, immediate areas for improvement. Work on advance planning (item a) can help you improve these.

Where to Go for Improvement Ideas

Each item on the survey is paired below with comments on relevant choices and tools for structuring more effective meetings. Choices are in bold and tools are in bold italics. See the *Tool Chest* for more information and directions.

Item	Relevant Choices and Tools
a)	Consider *How You Define the Work of the Meeting* (chapter 1). A group meets together most effectively when the work is clear to all and represents an effort to which all can contribute. Define the task(s) of the meeting clearly in terms of expected outcome(s) so that all know what needs to be done. The supporting tool for defining the work of the meeting I call by the acronym **FATT** (**F**ocused, **A**ctionable, **T**imely, **T**imed). Review *How You Plan to "Spend" Meeting Time* (chapter 5). Many meetings are criticized for being a waste of time. The difficulties often begin with unrealistic budgeting of the time available against the work of the meeting. Time management is made more difficult by the usual assumption that the meeting will continue as one linear, whole-group conversation. There are various techniques you can use to overcome these challenges and ensure that meeting time is well spent. The tool **Time Planning Tips** and **Time Planning Tips**^{VM} will help you design the meeting to spend time well.
b)	See above: *How You Define the Work of the Meeting* (chapter 1).
c)	Adding a few participants with different perspectives or responsibilities relative to the subject of discussion can produce more creative, complete, and easily implemented outcomes. See *Who Gets Invited* (chapter 2) for suggestions.
d)	See above: *How You Plan to "Spend" Meeting Time* (chapter 5) along with **Time Planning Tips** or **Time Planning Tips**^{VM}. For conducting the meeting, review *How You Manage Time* (chapter 10). Readjusting the "budgeted" meeting time for various items provides an opportunity to make the meeting as cost-effective as possible. The tool I call **Time Renegotiation** can be helpful here.

e)	See *How You Design the Discussion* (chapter 3 or Part IV for virtual meetings). Tools for designing the discussion so all can contribute no matter the size of the group include: **Go-Around, Go-Around**[VM]**, 1-2-All, PALPaR,** and **Hybrid Meeting Checklist**[VM]. When you are conducting the meeting, look to tools under *How You Support Productive Conversations* (chapter 9 or Part IV for virtual meetings).
f)	See above, *How You Plan to "Spend" Meeting Time* (chapter 5) and *How You Manage Time* (chapter 10), and particularly *How You Design the Discussion* (chapter 3) and *How You Support Productive Conversations* (chapter 9). The tool **PIP** (**P**resentations **I**n **P**erspective) may be helpful.
g)	Consider *How You Arrange the Meeting Space* (chapter 6). Different physical settings can support (or hinder) different types of conversations. Three tools can help you choose the best space, or find a better way to fit the space to your meeting's purpose: **Circle Up, Meeting Room Checklist,** and **Seating Structures.**
h)	See above for *How You Design the Discussion* (chapter 3). Also consider *How You Share Responsibility* (chapter 8). Sharing responsibilities also builds a sense of mutual responsibility for meeting process and outcomes.
i)	See *How You Intend to Reach Decisions* (chapter 4): Engaging everyone in the discussion means it is important to be clear, up front, about how decisions will be reached as a result of the discussion. There are five basic ways in which to engage others in decision making (only one of which involves counting votes): **Consensus, Consent, Compromise, Counting,** and **Consulting.** See **Five Cs** for more. Also *How You Build Decisions* (chapter 12): A step-by-step approach to building decisions can be used to respect different points of view and align participants around a common set of agreements.
j)	See summary above for *How You Share Responsibility* (chapter 8).
k)	*How You Manage Time* (chapter 10), summarized earlier.

l)	No specific tool.
m)	See *How You Follow Up* (chapter 13). Meeting outcomes can be implemented more effectively and consistently when people have an opportunity to plan their actions and reflect on subsequent results in an appropriately planned follow-up conversation. Tools include **Follow-Up Timing** and **Three Follow-Up Questions**.

Part VI

Meeting by Design, Not by Accident

**In the following chapters I present a variety of examples, sto-
ries, and suggestions about structural approaches to different
types of meetings.** Chapter 14 provides example designs to show
how structural tools can be applied in the context of some familiar
meeting situations. I show you the "blueprint" for how a meeting
is structured and also how the blueprint's details differ from the
public agenda used with the participants. Chapter 15 presents
examples of actual meetings structured to get work done in some
difficult circumstances. Finally, chapter 16 provides recommendations for structural approaches to a variety of challenges.

Chapter 14

Meeting "Blueprints" for Different Types of Meetings

I want to show you in detail how various choices and tools come together to structure a meeting that works. I provide designs for four different meetings which all reflect real and fairly common situations. One or more of these situations should be familiar, showing you how the choices and tools of a structured approach create an effective design.

Structure Reflects Function

The structure of any meeting should serve its function. Is the meeting intended to solve some problem, build a future vision, align team efforts, or something else? Different functions need different structures, and yet we often conduct all our meetings the same way—same participants, same location, same timing, same process for discussions.

For example, below are some familiar meetings with very different functions.

- **Staff meeting:** Typical function of such meetings is to connect members of an existing team or group to the ongoing work of the organization.

- **Problem-solving meetings (two examples):** Function of these meetings is to arrive at a decision that resolves some situation.

- **Meeting to build alignment and commitment:** Function here is to conduct a more effective leadership meeting after some difficult changes have occurred.

Each meeting will benefit from a particular structure that supports the nature of the work to be accomplished. I provide examples of how I would plan each of these meetings in detail—by sharing "blueprints" that show a structure to conduct them.

Planning a Meeting: Blueprints and Agendas

To plan a meeting, I outline its purpose and make choices to create an effective structure. I begin with the six choices for planning a meeting and also consider the choices for conducting and achieving results. As I make certain choices and select specific tools, I build a design or "blueprint" for how I intend to conduct the actual meeting. I then create a public agenda for participants, to inform them of the tasks and overall order and timing of the meeting. This public agenda is like the architect's drawing of the finished house; it presents a picture of the form of the house, but you don't see the detailed blueprints behind it. A good public agenda follows the form recommended by the **STARS** criteria. The blueprints, however, enable me to build and run the meeting as I intended.

Do I always recommend creating both a blueprint and an agenda? No. If this is a short or fairly straightforward meeting, I just create a clear, well-defined agenda for everyone to follow. It is likely that I will select several tools to create the structure, and I don't need to describe these for either the participants or myself. But I will create both a blueprint and an agenda for longer, larger, or more complex meetings. I know that I need to think through how I plan to conduct various activities, including timing for various steps and questions for guiding discussion. For these more complex meetings, spending extra time to think through how I intend to structure the meeting and create a blueprint to guide me is always worth it.

Sample Blueprints

The following blueprints are based on real situations. Hopefully they are familiar and you can recognize the relevance of the choices I made. My usual blueprints have two columns, with timing to the left of the description of the purpose and process of each step of the meeting. In the examples that follow, I have added explanatory notes in a separate column under "Comments" so you can follow my thinking. *This column would not normally be part of a blueprint I use to plan or conduct a meeting.*

I have also included an example of a participant or public agenda for the staff meeting. You can see how the agenda is related to the blueprint but presents a much simpler outline. In fact, to create an agenda, I usually do a quick "cut-and-paste" from the blueprint.

Finally, at the end of the chapter I include a section on common pitfalls in meeting design.

Staff Meeting "Blueprint"

Situation

This design is for a monthly staff meeting with the manager and seven participants. It follows the form for most of their monthly meetings. These meetings focus on no more than two or three discrete tasks to provide adequate time for the group to have the necessary discussion. Regular "updates" are not included in the meeting and instead are handled by email. Items that don't require the whole team's involvement are addressed in other, smaller meetings.

BLUEPRINT: Staff Meeting Agenda *(annotated)*

Timing: [90 minutes] 10:15 – 11:45

Time	Task/Item	Comments
10:15 – 10:25 (10 min)	**Check-In** Purpose: To give all a chance to speak and share what's on our minds as we arrive, so it can be set aside and we can be fully present for this meeting. (Manager) asks all to: • Check-in (1 minute (min) each). Just listen to each other. No discussion.	*Meeting starts at 10:15 so that everyone has time to finish any prior commitment and arrive on time to this meeting. See **Go-Around** for more on check-in.*
10:25 – 10:30 (5 min)	**Agenda Review** Purpose: Confirm that everyone understands the purpose of the items. • Check that there are no additional items to be addressed.	*Focuses participants on the work of this meeting.*
10:30 – 10:45 (15 min)	**Action Plans Follow Up** Purpose: To review and learn from progress on key actions undertaken since last meeting.	*Three people have action plans to review (5 minutes each).*

See **Three Follow-Up Questions** for more information.		Each person with an open action item provides brief update following this outline: • What has been accomplished as planned? • What has not been accomplished as planned? • What am I learning from progress so far?
Presenter or someone else may lead the group through the process: Information is reviewed in small groups around the table before the whole group discussion. See **Five Cs** and **1-2-All** for more on process used here.	**10:45 – 11:15** (30 min)	**Key Task for This Meeting** Purpose: Individual with responsibility for this item reminds group of intended purpose of this discussion, including how the group's views will be used in reaching a decision. Task leader makes brief presentation with handout (10 min), and then with manager leads the group through following steps: • Individual reflection (2 min) and discussion in pairs (8-10 min). • Whole group sharing of views discussed in pairs (10 min). • Final decision (5 min).
This is a small, simpler topic and so receives less time and processing.	**11:15 – 11:35** (20 min)	**Second Task for Meeting** Purpose: Responsible individual introduces task and decision. • Task leader presents issue and recommendation (5 min). • **Go-Around** to hear from all (10 min). • Final decision (5 min).
	11:35 – 11:40 (5 min)	**Action Planning** Review results and actions coming from meeting to make sure all understand the outcomes and next steps.
Updates have been limited here to make the best use of the whole group's time.	**11:40 – 11:45** (5 min)	**Closing** Share any final updates or reflections on meeting in a quick **Go-Around**. Updates should be important for the whole group to know.

An example of a public agenda for participants follows. By comparison to the blueprint, the agenda contains less detail on how the meeting will be conducted. This allows participants to focus on the work of the meeting rather than its process. The only exception is that the individuals leading the two main discussion items ("tasks") would need to understand the intended design (**1-2-All** or **Go-Around**) for those items in advance.

BLUEPRINT: Staff Meeting Agenda *(as shared with participants)*

Time	Task/Item
10:15 – 10:25 (10 min)	**Check-In** Purpose: To give all a chance to share what's on our minds as we arrive, so it can be set aside and we can be fully present for this meeting. (Manager) asks all to: • Check-in (1 min each). Just listen to each other. No discussion.
10:25 – 10:30 (5 min)	**Agenda Review** Purpose: Confirm agenda and purpose of all items.
10:30 – 10:45 (15 min)	**Action Plans Follow Up** Purpose: To review and learn from progress on key actions undertaken since the last meeting. • What has been accomplished as planned? • What has not been accomplished as planned? • What am I learning from progress so far?
10:45 – 11:15 (30 min)	**Key Task for This Meeting** Purpose: [Individual with responsibility for this item] will lead this discussion and help us reach a decision.
11:15 – 11:35 (20 min)	**Second Task for This Meeting** Purpose: [Individual with responsibility for this item] will lead this discussion and help us reach a decision.
11:35 – 11:40 (5 min)	**Action Planning**
11:40 – 11:45 (5 min)	**Closing**

Problem-Solving Meetings

Situation

Problem-solving meetings differ from staff meetings in more than function. A problem-solving meeting may bring together a varied group of participants in order to address all aspects of the situation. Also, while the task may seem clear, there may be very different views on what should be done. Particular attention should be given to such planning choices as:

- Who gets invited
- How you design the discussion
- How you intend to reach decisions

Blueprints for two different kinds of problem-solving meetings follow. (As before, the participant agendas would contain *much less* detail about the process of the meetings.)

Example One: Seeking Options

In this example, the leader convenes a group of ten to explore and decide on options to a current problem. The ten participants represent a range of responsibilities and perspectives on the problem. See the tool **Diagonal Slice** for more on how this group was assembled.

BLUEPRINT: Seeking Options Agenda

Timing: 75 minutes

Comments	Time	Task/Item
Sets context for this group's work and decision-making role. Important since this group does not normally work together and do not all have the same authority and status in organization, but the range of views is important to a good overall decision. Also see **Five Cs** *and* **Consensus Guidelines**.	**9:15 – 9:20** [5 min]	**Agenda Review** Purpose: Confirm the focus and intended outcome of the meeting. • Make sure everyone understands the focus/purpose of this meeting–the problem being addressed. • Explain why this group was assembled to address the problem. • Explain the intended means of making a decision with this group.

9:20 – 9:30 [10 min]	## Check-In Purpose: To give all a chance to speak and share a starting thought as they arrive. • Check-in (1 min each) by sharing a personal desire for the outcome of this meeting. • Just listen to each other. No discussion. After all have shared, thank everyone, and transition to the work of the meeting.
9:30 – 9:50 [20 min]	## Defining Criteria for a Successful Solution Purpose: To identify criteria for a successful resolution to the problem and agree on the priorities for those criteria. • Remind the group of the problem as defined and check that all understand it as defined (a pre-reading providing background on problem should have been sent out with agenda). • Lead the group in a "brainstorm" to identify possible criteria for choosing a successful solution. • Write the criteria on a flip chart as they are mentioned (time estimate: 5-8 min). When the list is complete, give each participant a strip of 4 self-adhesive dots and ask everyone to place dots on the criteria that are most important to him/her. Once the dots have been placed, ask the group to interpret the results: • What do you see in the pattern of our dots? • Are those with the most dots most important? Does this ignore something critical that just happened to get fewer dots? • And so on… (time estimate: 8-10 min).
9:50 – 10:00 [10 min]	## Identifying Specific Options for a Successful Solution to Current Problem Purpose: To identify a range of possible solutions to the problem. • Again ask the group to brainstorm, this time to build a list of possible solutions. • Remind people that this is just a brainstorm, not a time for discussing pros/cons of ideas. • A volunteer writes the suggestions on flip chart as they are shared.

Check-in gets everyone speaking and helps all to know one another and lessen concern for differences in status. Note that request is relevant, positive, and "safe." See Go-Around for more on check-in.

Here the leader builds the basis/criteria for any decision about the best solution before getting into any discussion over preferred solutions. This helps the group to build decisions that all can support. See **Visible Note Taking** *and* **Multi-Voting** *for more information.*

The precise number of dots can vary, but it's helpful to give each person 4 or more of the self-adhesive dots so that s/he makes more choices than just first, second, and third place.

10:00 – 10:20 (20 min)	**Choosing the Best Solution**
	Purpose: To identify a specific solution with group's support and commitment.
	Give participants strips of self-adhesive red and green dots and ask them to place a dot on each of the solution possibilities just identified.
	• Green dot means they believe that solution meets the most important criteria for a successful solution as identified in the previous discussion.
	• Red dot means they think that option fails to meet one or more of the important criteria.
	After all the dots have been placed, ask the group to interpret and resolve the pattern of dots:
	• Which option(s) received the most green dots?
	Assuming there are at least 1-2 red dots on even the "greenest" choice, the leader continues:
	• What do the red dots signify? Which criterion does this alternative fail to meet?
	• Is there some way to modify the option so that those red dots could be changed to green?
	After the red dots have been addressed and one option appears to meet all (or almost all) of the criteria for a successful approach, proceed to clarify the group's final decision. Ask for a **Go-Around** for each to share the nature of his/her support for this decision:
	• S/he gives it full support.
	• Or s/he can consent to this decision, as implementing it does not present any obstacles for his/her area of responsibility.
10:20 – 10:30 (10 min)	**Action Planning and Close**
	Purpose: To confirm outcomes and next steps.
	• Review decision and clarify next steps.
	• Thank everyone for his/her participation.

Leader does not ask who put up the red dots, but only what the red dots represent and how they might be resolved.

See **Multi-Voting** *for more information.*

Example Two: Improving Performance

In this second example of a problem-solving meeting, the leader convenes a group of 12 to see what can be done to improve performance on a goal whose achievement is in doubt. These 12 participants represent various perspectives and stakes in the goal's achievement. See the tool **ARE IN** for more on how this group was assembled.

BLUEPRINT: Improving Performance Agenda

Timing: 75 minutes

Time	Task/Item	Comments
9:15 – 9:20 (5 min)	**Agenda Review** Purpose: Confirm the focus and intended outcome of the meeting. • Make sure everyone understands the focus/purpose of this meeting–the problem being addressed. • Explain why this group was assembled to address the problem. • Explain the intended means of making a decision with this group.	*Sets context for this group's work and decision-making role. Important since this group does not normally work together and all do not have the same authority and status in organization, but the range of views is important to a good overall decision. Also see* **Five Cs**.
9:20 – 9:30 (10 min)	**Check-In** Purpose: To give all a chance to speak and share what's on our minds as we arrive, so these can be set aside and we can be fully present for this meeting. • Check in (1 min or less each) by sharing a personal wish for a successful outcome of this meeting. This is not a time for advocating a view. • Just listen to each other. No discussion. After all have shared, transition to the work of the meeting.	*Important to begin with a check-in to "break the ice" and make it easier for all to share their views through the meeting. Note that request is relevant, positive, and "safe." Also that this shouldn't be a time for advocating a position. See* **Go-Around** *for more on check-in.*
9:30 – 9:50 (20 min)	**Identifying Supports and Restraints on Goal Achievement** Purpose: To identify all the forces that participants see as impacting goal achievement. • Using the chart you prepared previously, explain that "supporting forces" are things that are currently improving the likelihood of achieving the goal. "Restraining forces" are those things working against the goal. • Explain that the middle line (the leg of the "T") is the current state. The group is going to consider how the various forces can shift the current state toward or away from achievement of the goal. Ask all to reflect for a moment and make individual lists of the supporting and restraining forces as they each see them.	*Tape 2 (or more) sheets of flip chart paper together on the wall to form 1 large work surface so there is plenty of writing space. Write the goal at the top and draw a "T" underneath with "Supporting Forces" on one side and "Restraining Forces" on the other. This can all be prepared in advance so little time is allotted here.* *See* **Forces Review** *for more information.* *Initial individual reflection helps all to think of more individual ideas before the group brainstorm.*

<table>
<tr><td>

Try to focus only on the supporting forces first. These may be more difficult to identify.

Some item(s) may seem relevant to both lists, having both positive and negative forces. This is OK.

You may want to have someone volunteer to be the note taker for this session. See **Visible Note Taking***.*

This process is not a comparison of arguments for and against something, but rather an exploration of what may be working in favor of or contrary to the desired outcome. It should be an open recognition of different views.

</td>
<td></td>
<td>

Then conduct the brainstorm:

- Begin with the "Supporting Forces" side. Ask group to brainstorm the supporting forces that (will) help in fulfilling the goal or recommendation under consideration. Remind everyone that this is a "brainstorm": all ideas are valid and there should be no cross-questioning of different ideas. As suggestions are offered, write them on the flip chart.
- After the suggestions drop off, turn to "Restraining Forces" and repeat the process. Write down the forces that are thought to hinder success.

</td></tr>
<tr><td>

These 6 dots allow each participant to "vote" for his/her opinions of the most important forces.

</td>
<td>

9:50 – 10:00

(10 min)

</td>
<td>

Identifying Most Important Forces

Purpose: To focus attention on the most important supporting and restraining forces.

- Give each person 6 self-adhesive dots. Ask each person to place dots on the 3 most important items on the "Supporting Forces" list and the 3 most important items under "Restraining Forces."
- Once all the dots have been placed, review the results and clarify what has been identified as the top 3 supporting forces and top 3 restraining forces.

</td></tr>
<tr><td>

This could be done as a whole-group effort, but in a larger group you will have more engagement and contributions if the group is divided in two, each half focusing on one "side" of the **Forces Review***.*

</td>
<td>

10:00 – 10:20

(20 min)

</td>
<td>

Identifying Possible Actions

Purpose: Choosing ways to work with the identified forces.

- Divide participants into two groups (by random assignment). One group will focus on Supporting Forces, the other on Restraining Forces.
- Focusing only on the top 3 supporting forces, ask participants to identify ways to strengthen each of these factors. In what ways can the forces working towards the goal be made still stronger in helping to achieve success?
- For the top 3 restraining forces, ask the group to identify specific ways to weaken each of these factors so that it is less of a barrier to success.

When both groups are finished, ask them to report out to each other, and clarify or build on the ideas as necessary.

</td></tr>
</table>

10:20 – 10:30 (10 min)	**Action Planning and Close** Purpose: To confirm outcomes and plan next steps. • Work with the group to determine overall conclusions and next steps. • What actions do participants want to implement (or revise and implement) in light of this review? • Where are the immediate opportunities to weaken some restraint or strengthen some support? • Which ideas will need a more detailed plan to be implemented, and who will complete that plan so action can begin? In closing, thank everyone for participation and ideas.

Track action plan decisions on the flip chart as they are reached so all can see them

Meeting to Build Alignment and Engagement

Situation

This example shows how meeting structure can be used to build greater cooperation, dialogue, and engagement in a group that is not working well together.

The meeting I outline here was a real one, although a number of details have been changed. It involved the board of a nonprofit organization. Such boards present some particular challenges in that they typically are large, with members who serve voluntarily and may not know with each other well. While your situation may not involve a board, many aspects of this meeting apply to any other large, loosely connected leadership teams with difficulty working together.

This board had been going through a difficult time. It normally had 20 members, but two members, one a long-time member and president, had resigned over a decision to fire one subcontractor and hire a new one. Various factions had developed and board members had become less open in their discussions with one another.

The former vice president took over as president. He was concerned that there were too many private exchanges and unspoken issues for the board to be able to work well together. Some members seemed to dominate board discussions while others held back and/or occupied themselves in other ways.

There was also a continuing concern for how the board used its meeting time. Board members had various committee responsibilities and board meetings were sometimes the only opportunity they had to talk together about some committee issues. Such committee work often made it onto the board's agenda—even if the issues did not involve the full board. Agendas had become unwieldy and unpredictable. Meanwhile, a special task force had been working on developing a proposed process for creating a new strategic plan. The new president wanted to make sure this proposal received the necessary time and attention at the next meeting so that the board could build broad understanding and alignment around its direction.

The president planned to use his first board meeting to begin changing how they got work done in these sessions. He made a number of structural choices and supported them with various tools. The blueprint below is the resulting design for that meeting. The meeting went very well and helped to realign this group while building support for the leader's new role.

As with earlier designs, I have added explanatory notes in the side column. I have also explained the process of the meeting in some detail in the middle column.

BLUEPRINT: Building Alignment & Engagement Agenda

Timing: 2 hours

Comments	Time	Task/Item
These rearrangements have been done to shift habitual seating patterns and create new possibilities for small-group interactions. See **Seating Arrangements** *for more information.*	**30 min** [before start]	**Room Set-Up and Seating Changes** The meeting room had usually been set up in 5 separate tables. This has been rearranged to form one large square. The 4 members of the executive team are asked to scatter their seats around the table. [President] sits in the middle of one side. A number of pieces of flip chart paper are posted at various places around the room.
His intent is to start on time while allowing 5 minutes for late arrivals. He is not trying to open up discussion yet, but rather to move on to the first real discussion in small groups. He chose not to use a **Go-Around** *[check-in] to avoid any potential for derailing the meeting at the start.*	**7:30 – 7:35** [5 min]	**Agenda Review** **Purpose:** Confirm the focus and intended outcome of the meeting. • Welcome everyone and make sure the agenda is clear. • Acknowledge some changes in how the meeting will be conducted and ask for support. [No discussion].

7:35 – 8:00 (25 min)	## Adjusting to Changes **Purpose: To acknowledge the recent difficulties and departure of the president and a board member.** Review the following 2 questions and ask all to turn to those beside them around the table to form groups of 3 (or 2) to discuss their responses. Give everyone 10 minutes for small-group discussion to make sure all can speak to both questions in their small groups. 1) What did you most appreciate about the efforts and service of Mary and Bill? 2) What opportunities and challenges does their departure represent for the board and organization? After 10 minutes, reconvene as a whole board by asking 3-4 of the small groups to share replies to question 1. After 3-4 groups report back on question 1, check with the other groups for additional/different comments. Once all the comments to question 1 have been shared, go around again to get replies to question 2. Begin with a different small group and repeat the previous process, making sure there is a complete list without a lot of repetitive reporting. Close this session, thank all for their sharing, and explain how to follow up on these opportunities and challenges in the coming months. Then transition to the next item.	*Intent is to provide a safe/open opportunity for people to share their reactions by first talking in small groups.* *Note: Mary was the president who left along with Bill, a board member.* *To save time and avoid repetition, he does not expect to hear from all groups each time. Instead, he samples the groups while making sure all key comments are noted.* *President begins to write key replies on flip chart as groups report replies on question 2.*
8:00 – 8:45 (45 min)	## Developing an Approach to a New Strategic Plan **Purpose: To provide input on developing a new strategic plan for the organization's next five years.** Ask the planning task force to present their initial recommendations for the need, nature, and development of an effective strategic plan. Ask them to outline their ideas in a 15 min presentation. Everyone is just to listen for now. At the end of the presentation, explain a process for gathering everyone's feedback. Task force makes its presentation with a supporting handout. As they finish, ask everyone to review the notes and turn to 2 or 3 others to form a small group. They are to discuss what they just heard and prepare their responses to the following questions: • What did we hear that we like? • Where do we need more information? • Where do we have concerns?	*The task force has been working for two months to understand what the organization needs in a strategic plan and how one could be prepared.* *This process uses* **PALPaR** *and helps to engage everyone in the process of developing the strategic plan in a helpful manner. Also see* **Three Reaction Questions**. *These small groups can be the ones used earlier, or slightly different ones.*

	They have 15 min to review the material and develop their replies. Then reconvene the whole board.
This process insures that all get a chance to share their views with others and get engaged in the thinking about how to proceed. It balances the input, and supports a thoughtful exchange within a defined period of time. Visibly recording the feedback demonstrates that it has been heard.	Ask various small groups for their replies to the first question. As the groups report, one of the task force members writes down the feedback on a flip chart.
	Ask each group for their answers to questions 2 and 3. A task force member again records the feedback where all can see it.
	Once all the feedback has been received, the task force members should thank everyone for their input. If there is some point that can be clarified right now, they can reply to it. Explain that the task force will take the rest of the feedback away for further consideration and come back to the next board meeting with replies and more information.
This is done to help the committees to reengage in their work. There has been considerable disruption to the board's work in recent months, because of both the holidays and the dissension. In future, any committee sessions will be conducted before or after the main board meeting. *There are 5 committees.* *He makes the task assignment very clear.* **Note:** *Specifying brief reports makes multiple reports possible. A lot can be summarized in 2 minutes if this limitation is known in advance.* *Some of the groups elect to stand around a flip chart page. Others choose to gather at one part of the table and lay the flip chart page on the table.*	**8:45 – 9:15** [30 min with prior set-up] **Concurrent Committee Sessions** **Purpose: To give board committees a time to meet, update each other, and plan their work.** Explain that they will now have an opportunity to meet in committees. Each committee is to: • Identify the most important next steps for their work in the next 6 months. • Identify any questions or resource needs that challenge their accomplishments. • Be prepared to deliver a brief (2 min) report to the whole board at 9:15. Remind them to consider the preceding discussion as the recent changes may suggest adjustments to their plans. Finally, explain that all have 30 minutes to meet in their committees. Each committee should have someone keep track of the time while someone else records key points on the flip chart to bring back to the whole group as their report. Ask committee chairs to choose a place to meet by a posted flip chart page around the room.
	9:15 – 9:25 [10 min] **Reports and Discussion** **Purpose: To provide a shared understanding of the work ahead.** Ask each committee for a 2 min report.

9:25 – 9:30 (5 min)	**Evaluation and Closing** Thank all for their contributions. Conduct a quick **Go-Around**, asking each person for 1 word that describes how they are feeling right now about how this board is working.

*This is a very quick **Go-Around** that does go slightly over the 9:30 end time, but this is hardly noticed. The comments are generally quite positive and several people use the term "Unity" to describe how they are feeling.*

Designing Your Next Meeting: Avoid These Common Pitfalls

All meetings are unique in some way. Hopefully, the preceding designs help you see ways to create better structures, but you still need to create your own blueprints. Here are four frequent pitfalls to avoid as you plan your next meeting.

Drafting the agenda before you plan the meeting.

Many of us try to put an agenda together before we have given much thought to the structure of the meeting itself. This is why I describe creating a **STARS** agenda as the very last step in planning—after having considered the various choices you want to make to design the structure of your meeting.

Putting the most important and most time-consuming items late in the meeting.

This can happen when the intent is to get many small items out of the way first. But this can result in running out of time for the more important subject that is now at the end.

Trying to fit too much into the meeting.

Meeting agendas often become too crowded, with limited time for real dialogue on the most important items. One way to avoid this is to move some items to a "consent agenda," where they get reviewed and approved as a group. You can also remove any "updates" by asking for written memos or reports to be shared in advance, with meeting time reserved only for questions.

Not allocating a realistic amount of time for discussion.

I often see an agenda with seemingly arbitrary amounts of time assigned to various discussion items. When I attend the subsequent meeting, it becomes clear that the timing was only general guidance; discussions run overtime and some agenda items get cut. As you plan the meeting, consider how many participants are present and make a rough estimate of the nature and complexity of the subject being discussed. If everyone is to contribute his/her thoughts, then allow at least one to three minutes per person. You can also plan to use some specific tools for designing the process of the discussion, which will give you an efficient and predictable use of everyone's time (e.g., **1-2-All, PALPaR, Go-Around**). See **Time Planning Tips** for more ideas on ways to plan the cost-effective use of time in meetings.

Finally, given all the time you have to spend in meetings already, you may be thinking that you can hardly afford more time to plan them. If so, I suggest you consider how many people will be in your meeting, and then consider how much more cost-effective the use of everyone's time would be if you had an effective structure. Improving the effective use of your participants' time could be the best return on your time investment of anything you do that day.

Chapter 15

Story Time: Examples of Meetings with Effective Structures

I want to share some detailed examples of how meetings in various circumstances have relied on structure to achieve better results. I begin with a story about improving a staff meeting in a manufacturing plant. This was a small group with some difficult personality dynamics. The second example describes structural changes for more productive discussions in a meeting run by Parliamentary Procedure. The final story focuses on one committee's efforts to engage community members in a difficult decision by changing the structure of public input sessions.

While these situations may not be like yours, they can help you see structural possibilities for your own meeting challenges. They also provide descriptions of various structural techniques in action.

Creating an Effective Staff Meeting with a Difficult Team

Situation

I was consulting to a management team from a food packaging plant. This team had managers of production, quality, customer service, maintenance, human resources, and engineering. Their style of participation in team meetings varied. The engineering manager was assertive and seemed to have a lot to say, while the quality manager always seemed to have additional ideas on most subjects. Other managers had little to say unless pressed. Given this uneven involvement, it is not surprising that some decisions reached in their meetings seemed to come undone later. The plant manager was frustrated with this pattern. She recognized that management meetings were often ineffective, particularly when decisions involved everyone.

We talked about her situation and I suggested several changes that could build balanced discussions and more alignment on decisions. She decided to implement some changes that would create a different structure for participation.

What Happened

On the agenda for the next meeting was a production scheduling decision. This involved an equipment upgrade that would halt production for a day and could create customer service and quality issues. The plant manager introduced the decision and explained that she wanted to arrive at a final plan that all could support, even if their support came with reservations. She then asked the engineering manager to present his plan.

After the plan was presented, the plant manager asked her whole team to take a few moments to gather their thoughts before any discussion. Then she asked them to turn to one other person around the table and discuss their views on three questions she had written on a flip chart:

1) What do you like about the plan?
2) Where do you need further information?
3) Where do you have concerns?

After the managers had shared their thoughts in pairs, she explained that she wanted to get a summary of their discussions. She asked the engineering manager not to reply to any points until all the comments were heard. Then, she went around the table and asked each pair to share their discussions about what they *liked* about the plan. Finally, she went around the table again and asked each pair to summarize what they had shared on the final two questions. As the pairs reported, she captured key points on a flip chart.

After hearing everyone's feedback, she asked the engineering manager for his replies. As he spoke, he provided clarifications and adjustments to his original plan. When he finished, other managers suggested ideas for actions that they could take to ease any negative consequences in their areas. The plant manager continued to record comments on the flip chart. As the discussion concluded, she conducted a quick go-around asking each manager if the plan had his/her support or if there were any remaining problems. All said they supported the plan, or at least consented to it, as they could manage any impact on their areas of responsibility.

The discussion lasted about 30 minutes and created a much stronger plan. The subsequent production rescheduling and equipment change went well. Afterwards, the plant manager commented that this success owed much to the better alignment of her team. She intended to use a similar approach with other complex team decisions.

Seeing the Structure of This Meeting

The plant manager wanted full participation in the final decision, and so she began by explaining that she was looking for everyone's consent, if not full support (see **Five Cs** for her options). This clarified expectations for some members who otherwise might have said little. Near the end of the meeting, she used a **Go-Around** to make sure each person could give their consent (or not) to the decision.

Creating a more balanced discussion was also important. To do this, she used the **1-2-All** process to support a respectful exchange of views, first in a small group and then across the team. **1-2-All** let individuals organize their thoughts before speaking and then speak initially to one other individual to clarify their reactions. Finally, she framed their small group discussion using a version of **Three Reaction Questions**. This made sure that positive reactions to the plan were heard across the team instead of focusing only on concerns.

The manager took several other steps to create a better structure for a thoughtful exchange. First, she asked the engineering manager to wait to hear all the comments before replying to any individual ones. This would give him time to gather his thoughts and hear a range of views before replying. It also meant that the usual pattern of outspoken advocacy by the engineering manager would be less likely to occur. The final discussion showed the benefits of this approach. The engineering manager had modified his initial plan and other managers contributed ways to help it succeed.

Another important change was how she supported the discussion by serving as discussion leader and note taker (using **Visible Note Taking**). She could have asked others to volunteer for these roles, but she was prepared to do this and so demonstrated her support for everyone's full participation. (See **Four Responsibilities** for more).

Supporting Efficient Discussion on a Difficult Decision

Situation

Some organizations run their meetings following Robert's Rules of Order, a form of Parliamentary Procedure. These rules promote the orderly conduct of meetings. Unfortunately, they can also hinder effective discussion and create "winners and losers" on decisions. But this need not always be the case. This next story shows the possibility for a structural approach to a meeting run by Robert's Rules.

The board of a small community nonprofit organization was facing a major challenge. They were midway through a major capital project when it became clear that the original budget was off by $250,000. Where would this additional money come from? Could the project be completed? And, how had this cost overrun happened in the first place?

The board explored various options and identified a set of combined financial arrangements they could take to cover this additional expense. However, according to bylaws, these plans would have to be approved by 75 percent of the organization's members.

A special meeting was planned. According to their bylaws, this meeting would follow Robert's Rules of Order. Board members were concerned that this could be a difficult discussion. A group of 80 or more members would have to understand the circumstances and the various options to arrive at a final choice. There was a good possibility that the meeting would focus on difficult questions and who to blame. The capital project committee would do its best to educate members, but no one could tell what would happen.

I asked the board whether we could try a different approach to structuring the discussion leading up to the vote. Robert's Rules sets up a pro/con discussion once a motion is on the floor. I thought it would help to engage everyone in discussion before making a motion.

What Happened

The room was set up in a semi-circle of several rows of chairs. Over 80 members arrived for the meeting anxious to determine what could be done about the funding crisis.

The moderator called the meeting to order and summarized the purpose and agenda of the meeting. He then asked the chair of the capital project committee for his presentation. The chairperson took the next 25 minutes to explain the history, progress, and current financial challenge along with options for addressing the challenge. This was an educational presentation and no motion was made. When the presentation ended, the moderator called for a "recess" and asked me to describe the next step.

I explained that this was an opportunity for everyone to share reactions and clarify questions to be addressed. I asked them to meet in small groups to identify one or two questions that they felt had to be answered before they could take a vote. This instruction was written on a flip chart where all could see it. I requested that they pull their chairs together to form small groups of approximately five people and encouraged them to turn to those they knew less well to have a richer discussion. I referred everyone to printed copies of the previous presentation and gave them 15 minutes to share their thoughts. The room was quickly buzzing with conversations.

When the time was up, I ended the small group discussions and called for everyone's attention. Using a microphone as a "talking stick" I moved around the room taking one reply from each group—one question they felt needed to be addressed. As they spoke, a recorder wrote each question on a flip chart at the front of the room where all could see it. I continued gathering questions from the various groups until all the questions, with no duplications, were listed on the flip chart. There were ten questions in all.

I turned the meeting over to the moderator who then called the meeting back to order under Robert's Rules. The chair of the capital project committee read the motion for the financing plan and the moderator asked him to begin the discussion by responding to the ten questions already raised. Once all the questions had been addressed, the moderator asked everyone for any further questions on the motion. There were none, so he took a motion and proceeded to the vote.

The result of this vote was unanimous approval for the proposal to resolve the financial crisis. Afterwards, people expressed considerable surprise at how easily this discussion had gone and how they appreciated the respectful way difficult points had been treated. Several people said they were glad they were able to talk with others in a small group instead of in front of everyone. Others commented on how pleased they were that everyone had been able to express their views and get answers to key questions. Board members told me that they felt the meeting took less time and produced a more considered result than they had anticipated.

Seeing the Structure of This Meeting

While I couldn't change the nature of Robert's Rules, I was able to create a different structure for several critical aspects of the meeting.

My first choice involved the arrangement of the meeting space. The traditional set-up would have filled the room with tables and chairs with two microphones at the front, one for the speaker and one for anyone who wanted to make a comment. (Some meetings go further to use designated "pro" and "con" mikes on different sides of the room.) I wanted to make changes to both the seating and the microphone set-up.

> **Seating.** I knew that any tables would get in the way of creating small discussion groups. It would be too hard for people to hear one another across a table with everyone talking; I wanted them to be able to pull their chairs together, knee to knee. I also wanted them to meet with people they knew less well and thought that the tables would make it harder to get them to move to talk with others. The flexibility of the moveable chairs could help mix things up.

> **Microphone.** I knew the microphone set-up had to be modified. In the context of a Robert's Rules meeting, it is common to have a fixed microphone on a stand where people can line up to speak once they have been "recognized." This creates a stilted environment. It can feel intimidating, or even adversarial to stand at a mike to address the moderator and the participants. Instead, I wanted a wireless mike that could be taken to participants so they could speak from their seats. This creates a greater sense of people speaking to each other from the middle of the group itself. (See **Meeting Room Checklist** for more on arranging a meeting space.)

I made these physical rearrangements so that I could take various steps to structure a productive conversation. The basic process I used followed the steps of **PALPaR** (for **P**resent, **A**sk, **L**isten, **P**ause and **R**eply). I knew there would be a lot of material presented and this would begin the process. I made sure there were printed notes so participants could refer back to key points. After the presentation, and the announcement of a "recess" from Robert's Rules, I asked participants to form small groups to discuss their reactions.

I also had to focus the work of the small group discussions to keep them on task and on time. I designed one simple task to guide this discussion: To identify the one or two key questions that need to be addressed to be ready to take a vote. This task fulfilled the **FATT** criteria for a clear purpose. I wrote it on a flip chart for reference once the groups started talking together and might need a reminder of the focus of their discussion.

When the time for small group discussion was over, I had everyone listen to the outcomes of the discussions by gathering one question from each group. I had a recorder write these questions on a flip chart as they were stated so all could see that their comments were recognized.

The next step in the **PALPaR** process (the "**Pause**") was brief. We ended the "recess" from Robert's Rules when all the group reports were complete. The chair of the capital projects committee had to be ready to reply quickly, but he had been able to gather his thoughts as the questions were first posted. This gave him more opportunity to organize his replies than the usual back and forth of a typical "Q and A" session.

There were two other changes that helped to structure a better exchange: the sampling of responses using the microphone and the use of **Visible Note Taking**. In using the microphone as a "talking stick," I chose one specific group to speak at a time. This helped to keep reports short and focused. I did not have to hear a report from every group if they could see that their question had already been mentioned and recorded on the flip chart. Recording the questions on the flip chart also helped to clarify meaning. Several groups seemed to have similar questions and I could check to make sure we all understood what a given group was asking.

Helping a Community Build a Better Decision

Situation

For my third story, I return to an experience I mentioned in chapter 1. This story involves creating a different structure for a series of meetings that broke a logjam on a difficult decision for this small New England town. Here's what happened.

Over the years, this community had used a standard approach to any critical decision. The town would form a committee that would meet for many months and bring a proposal to the annual town meeting for approval. In this case, the decision involved building a new school. How much would it cost? Where would it be located? Could an existing school be renovated for less money instead?

The town had struggled with this school building decision for ten years. Several committees had been formed only to have their proposals turned down. There were many opinions on how it should be built and what it should cost. Each time a committee developed a proposed solution, it failed to get the necessary support at town meeting.

This time, town leaders decided to try a different approach. They established a new committee made up of representatives of all the different viewpoints. This was a large committee (12 members), and if it was to succeed, the committee members would have to respect each other's ideas and avoid forming "sides." The task for the committee was clear: they had to develop a proposal for a new school that a majority of the town would support. But their process would be different. This committee would work to clarify options and build decisions a step at a time with town input helping to shape their choices.[xvii]

What Happened

I worked with the committee to plan a series of special "town forums" to engage the town in providing input to the committee's work. These forums would not follow the usual process of committee hearings. Specifically, they would not be held in the committee room. There would be no head table with the committee seated behind it. There would not be rows of chairs. And there wouldn't be a fixed mike where town people would line up to pose questions to the committee. Instead, we chose a space in one of the local schools. We set up this room with chairs scattered in small clusters with "exhibits" around the room presenting information and options relevant to the current decisions. We had several microphones we could pass around the room.

These forums were also different in how they were conducted. Each session began with a brief (10 to 15 minute) presentation by the committee chair. She explained the agenda for the evening and laid out the choices and questions to be explored that night. At the end of this presentation, everyone went to the various exhibits around the room for more information about points of interest to him or her. One or two committee members were at each location by a cluster of chairs. Up to this point, there was no general question and answer session. This would come next.

After spending 30 minutes in small group conversations, the whole group reconvened. All attendees, including committee members, were now seated in various places throughout the room. Microphones were handed around to allow different people to ask questions. Committee members responded to questions from wherever they sat. It became a citizen-to-citizen discussion.

Four of these forums, focusing on different issues, were held over many months as the committee's work progressed. Each forum attracted from 45 to 75 residents in addition to those watching local cable TV coverage or reading the very complete newspaper reporting. The committee arrived at its final proposal for the project just before the town meeting.

At the town meeting, the final proposal was explained and various town members lined up at the microphones to speak to the motion. A wide range of generally favorable comments came from various segments of the community, including those who had opposed earlier proposals. When the vote was held, the proposal was easily passed and a subsequent town-wide vote had more than 80 percent of residents giving their support.

Seeing the Structure of This Meeting

While this story is actually about a series of meetings, the core structural practices were all similar in how the:

- Work of each meeting was defined
- Discussion was designed and supported
- Meeting space was arranged, and
- Decisions were built step-by-step with the committee

Here's what these practices looked like.

Defining the Work of Each Meeting

Each of the community forums focused on a specific range of options, *before* the committee had reached its decision. This made it possible for the committee to remain open to new thinking and for the participants to provide clear, constructive comments. The forums never focused on evaluating a committee decision. Even at the last forum before the town meeting, the committee was soliciting feedback on three options. Keeping multiple options in front of the town as long as possible kept the ideas flowing and limited the development of "sides."

Designing and Supporting Discussions

A variation of **PALPaR** was the overarching structure for the forums. Each meeting began with a short presentation that explained what the committee had been doing and laid out the options under consideration in this session. Immediately after the presentation and without taking questions, participants moved to locations around the room where they could focus on some aspect of the project. One meeting, for example, reviewed options for the building site, and the break-out groups considered traffic patterns, opportunities for athletic fields, environmental impact, and so on. People could engage in more than one small-group discussion on different options over a 30-minute period. At the end of this time, everyone sat together as a group, with the committee members among them. The microphone was passed around as committee and community members shared their observations and questions.

Meeting Space Arrangements

The meeting space was selected and arranged to support interaction among community members. As I noted above, the forums were not held in a typical meeting or committee "hearing" room but rather in a flexible space where chairs and exhibits were easily rearranged. The usual symbols of power and authority (head table, rows of chairs in a "classroom" style, and a fixed microphone on a stand) were not present. This was to be a meeting of community members talking together.

Building Decisions Step-by-Step

Finally, the committee's process supported the gradual development of decisions. Differences of opinion were present, but the committee was able to use consent, consensus, or compromise (see **Five Cs**) to move ahead. Throughout our work, we avoided taking yes/no votes on an important decision until that decision was made and we needed a vote for the record. We did use **Multi-Voting** to explore preferences and see how different variables might be handled. On one occasion we also used **Forces Review** to work with all sides of an issue.

Additional Stories

I have shared stories of various meeting challenges in my blog at **www.meetingforresults.com/blog** as well as short examples throughout this book. Part IV includes a story about a virtual meeting. Part VII includes the story of a multi-stakeholder meeting designed to address a public health crisis.

Chapter 16

In Emergencies, at Least Try This

Leading effective meetings is not easy under the best of circumstances. How can you structure better meetings in challenging situations? In this chapter I explore some of the ways you can use structural approaches to improve discussions and decision-making when you face the following:

- **No time to prepare.** What's most important to do when you have no time to prepare?

- **Wandering discussions.** What can you do when a discussion is going nowhere fast—even if you are not leading the meeting?

- **Difficult conversations.** How can you structure more respectful meetings when you are addressing a contentious issue?

The final section of this chapter also lists the most relevant tools for use across five additional situations.

What's Most Important to Do When You Have No Time to Prepare?

A meeting is scheduled for 30 minutes from now to address some emerging issue. You simply have no time to think through the structural choices and tools to plan an effective meeting. What can you do?

There are various tools you can use to improve the effectiveness of a meeting almost on the spot.

To Define the Work of the Meeting and Plan How to Reach a Decision: **FATT And Five Cs**

These two tools help you and the participants to be clear about the purpose of the discussion. Clarifying the work of the discussion can be the most important thing you can do to improve its effectiveness and efficiency. Going further to define how you will involve this group in any specific decision will help the discussion and may improve later follow up. See the description of each tool for more information.

To Support Dialogue: **Go-Around, 1-2-All, Three Reaction Questions** and **Visible Note Taking**

These tools can be used to improve the quality of the group's exchanges with little if any advance notice. Both **Go-Around** and **1-2-All** engage everyone in the discussion and take little if any additional meeting time. There is also a version of **Go-Around**[VM] for virtual or hybrid meetings. (**1-2-All** is best used in face-to-face sessions.) **Three Reaction Questions** and **Visible Note Taking** (and **Visible Note Taking**[VM]) help you focus a discussion by encouraging balanced feedback and visibly recording suggestions.

What Can You Do When a Discussion Is Going Nowhere Fast—Even When You Are Not in Charge?

Does this sound familiar? You are in a meeting where the discussion seems to be going on without building towards a conclusion. You are not sure whether all the participants are even following the exchange. To top this off, you are only a participant yourself and not the leader of this meeting. You can't intervene to "fix" the discussion without taking on more responsibility than seems appropriate.

Even in this situation, there is still one tool you can apply to improve the discussion: **Visible Note Taking.** Explain that you'd like to track the progress of the group's discussion by keeping ongoing notes where all can see them. Then stand by the flip chart (or use your computer in a virtual meeting) and begin recording key points using the speaker's words as much as possible. This supports the group's memory of the discussion and shows how its decisions are evolving. Each participant can see that his or her comments are recognized. In other words, it helps the group see and "own" the progress of its discussion. If the discussion continues going in circles, someone will usually point to the notes and try to bring the group to some conclusion.

How Can You Structure More Respectful Meetings When You Are Addressing a Contentious Issue?

There are five tools that are particularly helpful in structuring a productive conversation when conflicts arise. You can plan to use most of these tools in advance of the meeting, but they also can be implemented in the moment when a discussion threatens to get heated.

1-2-All or **PALPaR** can be used in combination with **Three Reaction Questions** to create a more measured, balanced discussion. **1-2-All** is helpful because it asks participants to reflect first and then share their thoughts with one or two others before speaking to the whole group. These initial steps enable each person to gain insight into his/her own and someone else's perspectives. In addition, **1-2-All** can keep a discussion from being "stolen" by one impassioned participant as each person first shares ideas with one or two others. **PALPaR**, used with **Three Reaction Questions**, supports balanced feedback, and avoids the back-and-forth of question/answer that can seem like a verbal duel.

Forces Review and **Future Focus** are two tools that you can plan to use ahead of time, or adopt in the moment when a contentious situation arises. **Forces Review** can turn an unproductive debate into an exploration of both problems and possibilities. It engages the group in a constructive conversation about how to improve the possibilities of success while recognizing the difficulties. **Future Focus** keeps the group from rehashing past problems and puts the emphasis on the only thing anyone can affect, the future. I have seen **Future Focus** create a more positive exchange of views even when both parties were ready to go to court over a dispute on contract performance.

Which Tools Can Help You Address Other Specific Challenges?

Here are five additional challenging situations. Various tools for structuring effective meetings can be used alone or in combination to address them.

Very Large Groups of 15, 30, or More Participants

In such situations, the nature of the meeting space, the clarity of meeting tasks, and the ability for all to share their thoughts are critical.

Participants Have Little Alignment or Commitment to Follow Up on Decisions and Action Plans

This may reflect a lack of clarity about how decisions are being made and subsequent commitment to their success. To address this, specifically clarify how you wish to reach a decision with the group, and plan effective follow-up actions.

Poor Participation and Engagement in Discussions

This challenge can involve an ineffective agenda, poor presentations, inappropriate room set-up, and insufficient opportunities for participants to share their thoughts.

Meetings That Run Over Time on a Regular Basis

Poor time management can be due to an unrealistic agenda, unclear expectations for decisions, lack of ways to involve everyone in a discussion, and too little attention to planning and managing the use of time.

Virtual and/or Hybrid Meetings Where Participants are not in the Same Room Together

There are various challenges for effective virtual and hybrid meetings. These were discussed in Part IV, but it helps to be aware of some key tools.

The following table outlines the tools most useful in each of these situations.

Tools for a Variety of Challenges

A box is checked if a tool can help in this situation. This table is only intended as a quick reference to the most useful tools. Other tools may help you too, depending on the nature and purpose of your meeting. See Part IV for more on tools for virtual meetings, as well as an earlier section of this chapter for a discussion of recommended tools for contentious meetings.

Tools for Specific Challenges

Tool:	Large group	Lack of commitment to decisions	Poor engagement	Running over time	Virtual or hybrid
			Meeting Challenge		
1-2-All	✔		✔	✔	
80/20 Principle		✔		✔	
Affinity Grouping	✔		✔		
ARE IN		✔			
Circle Up			✔		
Consensus Guidelines		✔			
Diagonal Slice		✔			
FATT	✔	✔	✔	✔	✔
Five Cs	✔	✔	✔	✔	✔
Five Responsibilities^VM					✔
Follow-Up Timing		✔			
Forces Review		✔			
Four Responsibilities	✔		✔	✔	
Future Focus		✔			
Go-Around	✔	✔	✔		
Go-Around^VM					✔
Hybrid Meeting Checklist					✔
Meeting Room Checklist	✔		✔		
Meeting "Room" Checklist^VM					✔
Multi-Voting		✔			
PALPaR	✔		✔		
Positive Story Sharing (PSS)			✔		
Presentations In Perspective (PIP)			✔	✔	
Seating Arrangements			✔		
STARS	✔		✔	✔	✔
Three Follow-Up Questions		✔			

Tool:	Meeting Challenge *(cont'd)*				
	Large group	Lack of commit- ment to decisions	Poor engage- ment	Running over time	Virtual or hybrid
Three Reaction Questions			✔		
Time Planning Tips	✔			✔	
Time Planning Tips^{VM}					✔
Time Renegotiation				✔	
Visible Note Taking		✔	✔	✔	
Visible Note Taking^{VM}					✔

A Bit of Coaching

I suggest you keep two things in mind when implementing any of these tools in a meeting:

Plan Ahead if You Can

It is always better to plan ahead for how to structure part of the meeting using a particular tool and implementing the tool in the natural course of the discussion. Participants may feel manipulated if you adopt some tool on the spot in the middle of some difficult exchange. There are, however, some exceptions to this guideline, as some tools can be naturally adopted in the moment. Examples of such tools are **Go-Around**, **Multi-Voting**, and **Visible Note Taking.**

Just Begin

Don't emphasize the process that you are about to use. Just begin. People will accept your request to begin some activity but tend to resist being asked to follow some "process" when this is all laid out to them in advance.

Part VII

Why You Can Trust These Recommendations

The recommendations in this book are different from most prescriptions for running better meetings. How can there be a different way? Where does this approach come from? In short, can you trust it to work for you?

How can there be a different way?

Most advice for improving meetings falls into one of two schools. One school advocates adopting various rules or guidelines for how we should conduct a meeting. Examples of this approach include Parliamentary Procedure or the use of meeting "norms." In the heat of a discussion, however, rules are often ignored and guidelines forgotten. The other school recommends learning and applying more skillful behaviors for listening and talking together. Examples of such skilled behaviors include suspending judgment, speaking with data, asking open-ended questions, and so on. Unfortunately, such behaviors are hard for many of us to apply consistently, particularly in difficult conversations.

Fortunately, there is a third way to conduct better meetings. This one engages everyone in the work of the meeting while managing time and building commitment to outcomes. It doesn't require learning new behaviors and it works in difficult situations. This third approach uses *structure* to enable more effective discussion and decision-making. Since the 1980s, hundreds if not thousands of meetings have been run using a structural approach.

Where does this approach come from?

The recommendations in this book are based on relatively recent research into human behavior, particularly behavior in groups. Beginning in the 1940s, Kurt Lewin, Fred Emery, Eric Trist, and others built a foundation of theory and practice for working with group behavior. A few years later, Eva Schindler-Rainman and Ron Lippitt developed ways to engage whole communities in greater collaboration.

Beginning in the 1980s, organizational consultants began applying these ideas to large-scale meetings. Kathleen Dannenmiller, Fred and Merrelyn Emery, Harrison Owen, David Cooperrider, Dick and Emily Axelrod, and Juanita Brown contributed to a growing understanding of ways to create structures for productive conversation. Meanwhile, Marvin Weisbord and Sandra Janoff clarified structural principles underlying effective whole system discussions. The method they call "Future Search" is the basis of many of this book's recommendations.[xviii]

While there were improvements in large group meetings, there was less progress with the smaller meetings many of us attend every day—and find so frustrating. I wondered how large group, structural techniques might apply to these "regular" meetings run by leaders without a facilitation background. This book is the result.[xix]

Insights from a Difficult Meeting Made Easy

There was one particular meeting that caused me to begin thinking more about the advantages of a structural approach. In this meeting, the facilitators had to lead a difficult discussion among more than 100 people with different backgrounds, different roles and social status, and different languages. In spite of these challenges, participants had an effective discussion on a contentious subject and arrived at a common set of actions. Here's the story of that meeting.

Indonesia was experiencing a high rate of maternal mortality. A combination of factors contributed to the problem. One factor was that large sections of the country had few clinics staffed by doctors and nurses, and the medical establishment did not support the local midwives who were the only resource available to women in remote villages. There were also cultural and religious practices that added to the problems. Girls were sometimes married at a very young age and became pregnant before their bodies were ready. Also, women couldn't travel to get medical attention without their husbands, but their husbands were often gone from the village for weeks at a time to earn a living.

To address this problem, UNICEF decided to bring all the stakeholders together to agree on what could be done. The country's chief medical officer would be present along with various nurses, doctors, and midwives. Young women from two different villages and different local cultures would be present along with village and religious leaders. Finally, to support the ideas developed in this meeting, representatives of international relief organizations, donors, and the press were present. In all, there would be over 100 individuals. How could we manage the cultural, language, and status differences so all could participate? And how could we avoid having the meeting devolve into a series of presentations from the medical authorities?

I co-facilitated this meeting with Katharine Esty. We both came from the United States and spoke only English. Others would help us with translation, as four languages (at least) were being spoken in the room. We were using the Future Search design and the room was filled with 14 small groups organized by perspective (or totally mixed). Each group would manage its own work, often in the main language of the participants in that group. We just had to provide the right structure of clear task and time guidance. In such a large and diverse group, we really couldn't direct anyone's behavior. At one point I was standing by a wall covered with participant contributions, none of which I could read. Yet we were still able to help the group hold the conversation they needed to have.

After a two-day meeting, they had developed a set of conclusions that all could support and could use to begin addressing this complex public health challenge. From villagers to government officials, everyone was aligned and ready to move forward. The chief medical officer was quite surprised at the results and said that never in a meeting had he spoken less and learned more.

I began to reflect on my experience as I returned home. We had successfully applied a set of meeting practices in a very different cultural context. One key to our success was that these practices enabled us to direct the progress of the meeting without trying to control (or sometimes understand) individual behaviors. Structural techniques seemed naturally able to rise to the challenge.[xx]

As I thought about the meeting, I started to pose a question to myself: If structural techniques worked with large groups in challenging situations, could some of these techniques improve small group meetings? Shortly thereafter, I began working with colleagues[xxi] to explore this question.

Identifying Choices and Tools for This Book

In the 15 years since that Indonesian conference, I've been identifying practices of large group methods that are effective as stand-alone "tools" for everyday meetings. I have tested these practices and given them to others to lead their own meetings across a range of settings. I have also conducted workshops on the use of the tools with various groups of managers from different backgrounds. Through this experience I have learned what works and how others can adopt the tools and practices of a structural approach to their own needs and settings.

What I learned fell into two general areas. First, I recognized that large group methods came with a set of decisions about structure that are not always obvious to smaller, more everyday meetings. One example of this is the importance of defining a clear task for the group's work: A large group meeting won't work without a clear task, but we hold smaller meetings everyday without such clarity. Another example is meeting space: we give little attention to room arrangements for many meetings, yet room set-up has a clear impact on large group meetings. I eventually identified 12 structural choices that influence the success of many meetings.

My second area of learning was how various techniques can be organized by how they support the implementation of these 12 choices. I decided to refer to these individual techniques as "tools." There are a large number of these potential tools. Not all would be relevant or practical for leaders of smaller, everyday meetings. I tried to choose the most useful ones. Often I had to develop tools to support specific structural choices. I also had to make sure that any of the tools I recommended would work in the hands of most leaders in most situations.

I tried out the tools in different situations with various leaders. As I did so, I did the following:

- I identified the tools that could be applied from a simple set of instructions, as distinct from those that required a deeper understanding of group dynamics.

- I looked for those tools that were robust enough to work under less-than-ideal situations. Perhaps more important, they had to provide an obvious benefit in use.

- A few tools had to be adapted or even developed from scratch since nothing similar existed for large group meetings (e.g., tools for virtual meetings). These tools still had to support a more structural than behavioral approach to conducting the meeting.

- Finally, I realized how important it was that a tool had a certain "face validity" so that anyone could see how and why it would work. Leaders needed to be confident and comfortable in adopting tools for their meetings.

Over time, I defined and tested more than 40 tools that I edited down to the 32 in the *Tool Chest*.

Conclusion: Will a Structural Approach Work for You?

A primary purpose of this book is to spread understanding and application of a natural way to conduct more effective meetings. The practices presented here are not completely new or different. Early societies knew many of them (e.g., **Circle Up**). We just need to (re)discover how to meet together in ways that support more effective discussions. I encourage you to try out some of the ideas presented here in your next meeting and observe the results for yourself.

Part VIII

The Tool Chest

Various techniques and processes ("tools") can help you create an effective structure for your meeting. How to use each of these is described in this "Tool Chest."

The tools are presented in alphabetical order for ease in reference. Tools with the superscript "VM" are designed for virtual meetings.

The table below lists each tool and indicates which of the 12 choices it supports. Some tools support more than one choice as, for example, when they can help in planning as well as in conducting a meeting.

List of Tools and Choices

Tool Name	Planning	Conducting	Achieving Results
1-2-All Effective engagement for groups of any size.	How you design the discussion.	How you support productive conversations. How to work with any conflict.	
80/20 Principle Clarifying agreements.	How you intend to reach decisions.	How you support productive conversations.	How you build decisions.
Affinity Grouping Visualizing relationships among ideas.			How you build decisions.

Tool Name (continued)	Planning	Conducting	Achieving Results
ARE IN Identifying who should be present.	Who gets invited.		
Circle Up Supporting dialogue with the right physical structure.	How you arrange the meeting space.		
Consensus Guidelines Reaching consensus decisions effectively and efficiently.	How you intend to reach decisions.		How you build decisions.
Diagonal Slice Selecting participants to represent the whole organization.	Who gets invited.		
FATT Defining a clear meeting task–**F**ocused, **A**ctionable, **T**imely, **T**imed.	How you define the work of the meeting. Also see **STARS** agenda.	How you manage time.	
Five Cs Choosing how to decide with a group–**C**onsensus, **C**onsent, **C**ompromise, **C**ount, **C**onsult.	How you intend to reach decisions.		How you build decisions.
Five Responsibilities^{VM} Sharing the work of running a virtual meeting.	How you plan to "spend" meeting time.	How you share responsibility. How you manage time in virtual meetings.	
Follow-Up Timing Choosing the best time to learn from actions.			How you follow up.

Tool Name (continued)	Planning	Conducting	Achieving Results
Forces Review Talking constructively about both sides of an idea.		How you support productive conversations. How to work with any conflict.	
Four Responsibilities Sharing the work of running the meeting.	How you plan to "spend" meeting time.	How you share responsibility. How you manage time.	
Future Focus Working on the desired future rather than past problems.		How you work with any conflict.	
Go-Around Hearing from everyone present.	How you design the discussion.	How you support productive conversations.	
Go-Around^{VM} Hearing from everyone in a virtual discussion.	How you design the discussion.	How you support productive conversations.	
Hybrid Meeting Checklist Working with remote and local participants.	How you arrange the virtual meeting space.		
Meeting Room Checklist Providing a physical setting to support the meeting.	How you arrange the meeting space.		
Meeting "Room" Checklist^{VM} Providing an effective physical setting for virtual meetings.	How you arrange the meeting space.		

List of Tools and Choices

List of Tools and Choices

Tool Name (continued)	Planning	Conducting	Achieving Results
Multi-Voting Showing patterns of preference.		How you support productive conversations.	How you build decisions.
PALPaR Creating a respectful exchange in response to some proposal. **Present, Ask, Listen, Pause and Reply**	How you design the discussion.	How you support productive conversations. How you work with any conflict.	
Positive Story Sharing (PSS) Building understanding of common experiences.	How you design the discussion.	How you support productive conversations.	
Presentations In Perspective (PIP) Ensuring that presentations support discussion.	How you support productive conversations.		
Seating Arrangements Changing interaction by changing seating.	How you arrange the meeting space.		
STARS Creating one plan to manage all—**Specific, Timed, Actionable, Relevant, Shared.**	Agenda tool summarizes all PLANNING choices for use in CONDUCTING the meeting.		
Three Follow-Up Questions Learning from a balanced review of progress.			How you follow up.

Tool Name [continued]	Planning	Conducting	Achieving Results
Three Reaction Questions Gathering balanced feedback.		How you design the discussion. How you work with any conflict.	
Time Planning Tips Planning and managing a scarce resource.	How you plan to "spend" meeting time.	How you manage time.	
Time Planning Tips[VM] Planning and managing a scarce resource in virtual meetings.	How you plan to "spend" meeting time.	How you manage time.	
Time Renegotiation Keeping everyone responsible for managing time.	How you plan to "spend" meeting time.	How you manage time.	
Visible Note Taking Recording the progress of the group's discussion.	How you design the discussion.	How you share responsibility. How you support productive conversations. How you manage time.	
Visible Note Taking[VM] Recording the progress of the virtual meeting discussion.	How you design the discussion.	How you share responsibility. How you support productive conversations. How you manage time.	

List of Tools and Choices

1-2-All

Effective Engagement for Groups of Any Size

What Is It?

1-2-All is a simple process that gives everyone a chance to organize and share his/her thoughts. You can use this tool anytime during a meeting when an important new question or proposal is introduced and you want to provide all with a chance to contribute.

Why Use it?

1-2-All helps you address various barriers to full participation.

- You have a large group (more than 8).

- You expect that some people may tend to monopolize discussions.

- You feel that some people may refrain from speaking to the whole group because of differences in status or perspective.

- You are concerned about managing discussion within the available time.

- You need to work with differences in language fluency.

How to Apply **1-2-All**

After introducing a subject or question to be addressed by the group, complete the following steps:

1   **Individual Reflection.** Check to make sure everyone understands the question or topic for consideration, and

then give individuals one to two minutes to gather their own thoughts. (This is the "**1**" of the tool.)

2 **Small Group Discussion.** Next ask participants to turn to their neighbors to form small, two to three person groups to share their ideas. Explain the time they have for their discussion and ask them to make sure everyone in their small group can share his/her thoughts in that time.

All **Report to Whole Group**. Ask each group for a brief report (typically one to three minutes) summarizing key points from their discussion for all to hear. Further discussion follows once everyone has heard from the small groups.

Tip: Plan how people will be seated. It may not help if participants share their thoughts in a small group of their closest associates. If you plan ahead you can ask people to sit with those they know less well *as they arrive*. See the tool **Seating Arrangements** for more information.

Tip: Set a specific length of time for small-group reports. Usually one to two minutes is enough. Ask groups not to repeat points already made.

Related Tools and Information

Another tool that helps balance participation is **PALPaR. 1-2-All** also works well paired with **Three Reaction Questions.**

80/20 Principle

Clarifying Agreements

What Is It?

This principle refers to a common, but often unrecognized, characteristic of many group deliberations—the tendency to focus on areas of disagreement. It can be used to help a group focus on the 80% on which they agree and can make progress.

Why Use It?

Most groups put much of their time and energy into discussing areas of disagreement. This may be only a few small points, perhaps 20% or less of the total subject under consideration. They subsequently fail to give attention to the majority of the subject on which they do agree and where forward progress is possible. This tool makes this tendency visible and asks the group to reverse the usual pattern by focusing on agreements and action plans for the 80% where they do agree and respectfully setting aside the 20% of the subject where they don't agree. They can return to the unresolved issues later—issues that may look very different after initial accomplishments.

How to Apply the **80/20 Principle**

Introduce the **80/20 Principle** to participants along with how you expect to arrive at decisions from this meeting. Say something like this:

> *"In many situations, a group agrees on 80% of the area under discussion, and disagrees on only 20%. But they get*

stuck on that 20%. Rather than get stuck, I recommend we look for the areas of agreement and see what action may be possible. And I suggest we respect but not devote all our attention to areas of disagreement. Once we begin work on some areas, we can see how the 20% may be resolved in the future."

- Explain that any areas of disagreement will be *acknowledged* and respected, but ask that they not become the focus of the group's discussion. To be "acknowledged" means that any disagreement will be recorded as part of the group's work as something that has not been resolved and will require further attention in the future.

- Explain that you are not looking for exactly 20% disagreement. It is just a generalization based on experience.

When the group begins debating some disagreement, remind them of this principle and suggest that this point be noted as not (yet) agreed and ask if it's OK to move on. **Visible Note Taking** is helpful so all can see their points (agreed or not) have been recognized.

Tip: Introduce this principle before you get stuck. You should introduce this principle early in the meeting if you think it may be relevant. It works best if participants understand it in advance. Don't wait until you get stuck or it may seem that you are trying to downplay someone's concern.

Related Tools and Information

Related tools include **Consensus Guidelines,** as this principle can help a group recognize consensus. **Future Focus** and **Three Reaction Questions** are other means of building decisions with a group in a productive way. The **80/20 Principle** may also be useful when using **Multi-Voting** by helping the group recognize its ability to move ahead.

Weisbord and Janoff (2010, 87) describe this principle and its value more fully as "confirming common ground."

Affinity Grouping

Visualizing Relationships

What Is It?

Affinity Grouping is a process for organizing diverse ideas to help a group recognize similarities and differences among suggestions.

Why Use It?

When you expect to generate a range of ideas or considerations, it helps to keep track of individual suggestions and develop a visual "picture" of the relationships among them. This respects individual contributions and gives everyone an understanding of how ideas may relate to one another.

How to Apply **Affinity Grouping**

If you expect to generate many ideas in a discussion, begin taking notes on large sticky notes, one idea or comment per sticky note. Use a dark marker that won't bleed through the paper. You can also have participants write their own ideas, one to a sticky note, also using dark markers.

Post the notes in any order on a clean surface with plenty of room for moving the notes around.

When the group has begun to run out of suggestions, ask everyone to organize the information they have just generated into groups of similar or related ideas.

Give the group some "rules" for this activity:

"Anyone can move a note at any time to another location. Notes can be moved more than once."

"No talking." (This is an organizing activity, not a debate.)

"You can create a duplicate note if you need one idea in two places."

Once the group stops moving the notes around, have everyone sit or stand where all can read the clusters and lead a discussion:

"What is a good label for each cluster?" (Put the label on the clusters.)

"What are we learning about the decision from this clustering?"

You may want to follow this with **Multi-Voting** if relevant to building your decision.

Related Tools and Information

Multi-Voting is useful in helping the group establish priorities among the clusters of items.

ARE IN

Selecting Participants to Represent the Relevant System

What Is It?

The **ARE IN** acronym, developed by Weisbord and Janoff (2010), reminds you to consider all those who should be present at the meeting, given the work and intended results. It causes you to consider including representatives across the whole system to be affected by this discussion.

Why Use It?

Including a range of participants having relevant information and experience can lead to more insightful and effective decisions. This tool also highlights the importance of including those who will have to implement, or may be affected by, any decision reached.

How to Apply **ARE IN**

Be clear about the work of the meeting and what a successful result will entail. Then plan how to include those who represent one or more of the following:

- **Authority** to act on meeting conclusions.
- **Resources** to apply in implementing meeting conclusions.
- **Expertise** on critical aspects of the discussion or decision.
- **Information** on some aspect of the discussion.
- **Need** for an effective outcome of this meeting.

While it may not be realistic to have someone representing "**Need**" present, you may find some way to include their *representatives*. Or you may be able to include information from them, using their own words.

Related Tools and Information

Both **ARE IN** and **Diagonal Slice** are ways of selecting a range of participants as relevant to the work of your meeting. Each has a different emphasis. They both encourage you to think beyond the "usual suspects" to create a meeting that can generate new insights and broader support.

For more information on **ARE IN**, see Weisbord and Janoff (2010, 110-111).

Circle Up

Using the Most Powerful Structure for Productive Discussions

What Is It?

Circle Up is a reminder to arrange your meeting space in a circle, or as close to a circle as possible.

Why Use It?

How we are seated in a meeting can reflect relationships, hierarchy, and influence. Sitting on different sides of a table can create a sense of sides in the discussion.

Being seated in a circle creates a more balanced conversation. By definition, a circle is a shape that has no sides, does not have a head, and allows all positions to be equal. Participants can see everyone easily. Conversation flows more naturally when each person in the group can make eye contact with every other person.

How to Apply **Circle Up**

Plan to seat people in a circle or as close to a circle as possible. Usually this means using a round table. If only a rectangular table is available, consider removing the table entirely and seating people in a circle of chairs. Participants will soon get used to working together without a table in front of them.

If you simply can't set up a circle, the second best choices are either a semicircle or a square table. If you have a large group, you may need to set up an oval, or concentric rings of chairs.

Avoid classroom style seating (rows of chairs) or a big "U." Such arrangements create power positions and send a subtle message that people are here more to listen than to engage with each other.

Related Tools and Information

Meeting Room Checklist and **Seating Arrangements** provide additional guidance on room arrangements. For more information on the importance of sitting in a circle, see Baldwin and Linea (2010).

Consensus Guidelines

Practical Approaches to Consensus Decisions

What Is It?

Consensus means reaching a decision that all support. If someone has an objection to something under consideration, then consensus has not been achieved. Consensus also means that the opinion of each participant is equal to others. **Consensus Guidelines** helps you achieve this type of decision.

Why Use It?

Consensus can be a practical and powerful form of decision making with a group if you approach it in an effective way. Unfortunately, it is often poorly done. As a result, many of us see it as time-consuming or impractical to achieve. Some discussions may default to "pseudo-consensus." In this case, consensus is assumed but perhaps weak and untested—unless someone takes the (risky) step of challenging the presumed decision.

How to Apply **Consensus Guidelines**

There are two ways to achieve consensus with a group. You can use either one or both in combination.

Option 1: Clarifying Agreement and Respecting Disagreement

Often it is possible to achieve consensus on most aspects of some proposed decision, but there are a few "sticking points" that keep it from achieving complete support. You may be able to achieve consensus on part if not all of the decision by separating points where there is consensus from those where there is disagreement.

- Specific areas of agreement are defined and separated as necessary from those points that are not agreed by all.

- Areas of disagreement should be defined, recorded, and respected as areas "not (yet) agreed." These areas can be revisited in the future as work begins on implementing the areas where there is initial agreement.

This process depends on effective use of **Visible Note Taking** so that all can see the points agreed, and/or points set aside as not (yet) agreed.

Option 2: Building Consensus by Go-Around

This approach begins with one person presenting the proposed decision. Anyone may ask a clarifying question as needed. The process to achieve consensus then goes as follows:

1) **Reaction round:** Lead a **Go-Around** to hear each person's reaction to the proposal. A brief (30-second) comment from each person should be enough. This is not a time for additional proposals or amendments nor is it time to go back and forth between two or more of the group members.

2) **Revising the proposal:** The person making the original proposal can now revise it based on all comments received and present the revised proposal back to the group.

3) **Clarifying objection round:** Next, go around the group again and ask for any objections to the revised proposal. Objections must be based on a personal concern or interest and explained to the group.

4) **Improving the proposal:** As a group, discuss how to improve the proposal, or remove parts of it, or include precautions or limits to the proposal. Complete any revisions.

5) **Final round to check that there are no more objections:** Once again go around the group to give each person a chance to speak briefly about their support or concerns with this last version of the proposal. This is not a time

for debate, but an opportunity to verify that there is (or is not) consensus given the revised/improved proposal. As relevant, identify and record the decision and any action items.

A consensus decision-making session should always end with a "no-objection" round to clarify the nature of the group's final consensus decision. If agreement has not been reached on all aspects of the proposal, this final no-objection round can be to confirm that all support some aspects and to clarify those areas where disagreements remain (per Option 1 above).

Related Tools and Information

Related or supporting tools include: **Go-Around, 80/20 Principle, Visible Note Taking**. For further information on how to make consensus practical using Option 1, see Weisbord and Janoff (2010, 59-60). For more information on Option 2, see Buck and Villines (2007).

Diagonal Slice

Selecting Participants to Represent the Organization

What Is It?

This is a simple tool for identifying a cross-section of possible participants from the organization or community. This tool does not presume any particular number of participants in the meeting.

Why Use It?

Consider inviting participants across a "diagonal slice" of the organization when you want to have diverse views and experience as part of the discussion. After the meeting, such a varied group of participants also improves the likelihood that others will support the conclusions reached.

How to Apply **Diagonal Slice**

- Be clear about the work of the meeting.
- Look across all levels, functions or interests in the organization or community and invite participants from each level and function.
- To manage the size of your meeting, you do not have to invite all levels from each function. Instead consider whether a given participant can represent both his/her function and the perspective of a particular staff level across the organization.

- You may want to double-up on participants from some group that has little power or influence. This helps to ensure that those with less status in the organization feel comfortable contributing their thoughts in front of others.

Related Tools and Information

Both **ARE IN** and **Diagonal Slice** are ways of selecting a range of participants as relevant to the work of your meeting. Each has a slightly different emphasis. They encourage you to think beyond the "usual suspects" to create a meeting that can generate new insights and broader support.

FATT

Defining a Clear Task:
Focused, Actionable, Timely, Timed

What Is It?

A meeting is usually held to accomplish some task with a group. **FATT** describes how the task can be defined to engage participants effectively in this work. There can be more than one task to be accomplished in a meeting, but each should be:

- **Focused:** The subject for discussion is a clear and bounded task so everyone understands exactly what is under consideration.

- **Actionable:** The decision to be reached can be acted on by those present. This group has the relevant authority, resources, and information.

- **Timely:** This is the right time to address this topic.

- **Timed:** An appropriate amount of time is assigned to complete the task.

Why Use It?

The more clearly the task description fulfills the **FATT** criteria, the more likely it is that the group will engage each other effectively in the work of the meeting.

A good **FATT** statement is like a "fat pitch" in baseball—a pitch that is right across home plate and easy to hit. A clear task statement helps meeting participants get a solid "swing" at a piece of work. Example: In response to a safety incident, a management team might meet to discuss "Yesterday's safety incident." A more clearly focused task is "What can we learn from yesterday's safety incident that we can apply to improve workplace safety going forward?"

How to Apply **FATT**

As you develop your plan for the meeting, define or review each main task against the following criteria:

Focused: Each significant piece of meeting work should be clearly defined, along with any necessary boundaries on the scope of the discussion.

- You may want to frame the work in terms of a desired future achievement, as this can build more energy and creative thinking.
- You can also focus the discussion by posing the work as a question.

Actionable: You should describe the task in such a way that participants will see it as one for which they have knowledge and authority to act.

Timely: It should be clear that this is the best time to address this topic. If it isn't important to address now, it shouldn't be on the agenda.

Timed: You should specify adequate time to accomplish this task, given the expected discussion and number of participants.

Tip: Updates. If you have general "updates" as part of your agenda, consider whether these are work you need the group to do together or whether information sharing is better handled by some other means.

Related Tools and Information

As you develop your task statement(s), they become part of a **STARS** agenda.

Five Cs

Choosing How to Decide

What Is It?

Five Cs clarifies the various ways that decisions can be reached with a group so that you can choose one that fits the task and communicate this to participants.

Why Use It?

An effective meeting should build alignment and commitment to any decisions. Different approaches to reaching decisions can be more/less useful in building commitment. Unfortunately, some leaders don't make a conscious choice of decision method and don't explain their choice to meeting participants. This can create various difficulties. For example, participants may assume they are providing input to the leader's decision, while the leader assumes s/he is gaining their complete support. Such confusion can lead to inappropriate expectations, difficult conversations, and poor results. To avoid this, plan how you will reach a decision on any given meeting task, and communicate the intended approach to the meeting participants.

How to Apply **Five Cs**

Choose how to decide in advance, by selecting the method appropriate to a given task in the meeting. Communicate how you expect the decision to be made to the participants at the beginning of the discussion.

- Some situations call for a combination of approaches. For example, a meeting may require a formal vote "for the record," but this vote could be a last step after the group has reached a decision by some other means (i.e., consensus, consent, or compromise).

- Sometimes you may want to have a back-up method of decision making in case your initial choice becomes unworkable in the meeting itself.

The five basic approaches to reaching a decision with a group are:

Consensus: Set the expectation that the group will develop a common conclusion which all will support. If one person has an objection, then you don't have consensus. You may plan to agree to disagree by separating areas of consensus agreement from areas of disagreement, respecting the latter areas as "not (yet) agreed."

Consent: Explain that in reaching consent, everyone should comment on the decision. Each person indicates whether s/he supports it or has a fundamental concern that this decision will have a negative impact on something critical to his/her responsibilities or customers. Explain that by consenting to some decision, each person is saying that s/he can live with the decision. It does not have to be perfect, but "good enough."

Compromise: Everyone gives up something s/he wants to achieve a unified common outcome. The decision is good enough for everyone, although some may say that they wish it had been somewhat different.

Count: This is decision by majority rule. The decision is reached in favor of the alternative or proposal that receives the most votes. Some win and some lose. While presumably simple to use, this approach poses challenges for effective deliberation, even when no obvious vote is taken.

Consult: Here you ask for the group's input to shape some decision you are about to make. You can propose a likely decision and some options, and then gather the group's reactions. Be clear about your process and how much influence the group's comments are likely to have on your final decision. This is an effective approach when you want to test some draft decision with the hope of modifying and improving it before deciding on its final form.

Comparing Approaches

Each approach to decision making has certain strengths and weaknesses. You should consider these when selecting an approach for a given task.

Consensus: Clear agreement by all (including an agreement to set aside any disagreement on certain aspects if necessary).

➕ Broad engagement and commitment of all participants to the decision.

➖ Can be ineffective if not properly managed. Use of **80/20 Principle** may help group to work with agreements and respect disagreements.

Consent: Each person confirms the group's decision unless s/he has some fundamental objection.

➕ While some participants may be more supportive of the decision than others, all must specifically give their support.

➖ Can be ineffective if not properly managed. Need to be clear about the true meaning of consent.

Compromise: Each party to the decision gives up something to meet half-way and arrive at a decision both will support.

➕ One broadly supported decision is reached in spite of multiple, possibly conflicting positions on what the decision should be.

➖ Some participants are likely to feel they had to give-up too much in order to reach closure. Decision may not be well-supported.

Count: This is majority rule based on counting votes. The option with the most votes is the one chosen.

➕ One decision is reached in spite of multiple positions on what the decision should be. Can be efficient.

➖ Can be ineffective as it may only achieve compliance, or something less, from those who feel that his/her "side" lost.

Consult: Person with overall accountability makes the final decision after receiving input from the group.

➕ Final decision may be improved with the group's input. Also, can create more support and understanding of the eventual decision.

➖ Needs to be handled openly and honestly, not suggesting more opportunity for influence by the group than is realistic.

Related Tools and Information

Other relevant tools include **Consensus Guidelines** and the **80/20 Principle** for consensus decisions, and **PALPaR** for a decision where you want the group to consult on a final decision to be made by the leader. The process of reaching decisions by consent is well described in Buck and Villines (2007).

Five Responsibilities^{VM}

Five Responsibilities^{VM}

Sharing the Work of Running a Virtual Meeting

What Is It?

Five Responsibilities^{VM} describes five responsibilities that need to be fulfilled to varying degrees for an effective virtual meeting.

Why Use It?

The responsibilities for an effective discussion are often over-looked, or left to one person (e.g., meeting leader) to cover. This is a particular challenge when the leader is the person who has a lot to say on a subject. Giving different responsibilities to individual participants means that each responsibility can be better managed. Dividing up these responsibilities also creates a sense of shared ownership for meeting outcomes.

How to Apply **Five Responsibilities**^{VM}

Before the start of a virtual meeting, get agreement from individuals to take on the responsibilities listed below. Do this before the meeting to give them a chance to become familiar with any technology and learn who will be participating.

Discussion leader: Responsible for making sure each person who wants to contribute can do so in the time available. The role of discussion leader may switch from one person to another. It is best to separate this role from that of the person responsible for presenting information or making the decision. Maintaining a balanced discussion is particularly challenging in a hybrid virtual meeting where some of the participants are together in a room where they may speak and interact with each other more often than is true for the remote participants.

Timekeeper: Keeps track of the time available. As the meeting proceeds, the timekeeper alerts the group on progress against remaining time. When necessary, the timekeeper may raise a question about changing the agenda if it appears that more time may be needed for a particular discussion.

Recorder: Uses any of a variety of means to record the progress of the group's discussion where all can see it. This can mean using a shared screen visible to meeting participants, or a flip chart and camera to share the notes via Skype, or a shared document like Google Drive. See **Visible Note Taking**[VM].

Information manager/minutes: Maintains the formal documentation and recorded minutes of the group's work.

Technology minder: Makes sure the meeting technology is working as needed. This person should test the technology in advance and become familiar with what to do if there is a problem during the meeting. The technology minder should also make sure that all participants can connect. If a problem arises during the meeting, the technology minder can work on the problem while the meeting proceeds if possible (by audio only).

Make sure each person understands the scope of his/her responsibility for this virtual meeting. All should be able to participate in the discussion as well as cover one of these roles, but you may need to rotate roles to help them do so.

Related Tools and Information

Supporting tools include **Go-Around** and **Visible Note Taking**[VM].

Follow-Up Timing

Choosing the Best Time to Learn from Actions

What Is It?

Follow-Up Timing provides guidance on when any follow-up discussion should occur for greatest effectiveness. This guidance is based on how we naturally manage our feelings and attention to complete and incomplete tasks.

Why Use It?

Many meetings end with some plan for follow up, which may be scheduled for some convenient future date—sometimes months ahead. However, it is important that the follow-up conversation happen sooner rather than later if the action items are more than simple tasks to be checked off some list.

We all tend to respond differently to complete and incomplete tasks. Most of us tend to forget what we have accomplished. Once something is done, we give it little further attention. By comparison, we are often quite aware of what we have not done as planned. Unfulfilled responsibilities create internal tension. We then (unconsciously) adopt some means of reducing this tension. Often this means developing an explanation for just how unrealistic it was to complete the planned action. However, if we reflect on progress while initial accomplishments are easy to recall and while internal "excuse-making" for anything incomplete is not too ingrained, then we can learn from experience and revise plans for continuing the work.

How to Apply **Follow-Up Timing**

Plan and announce a review of progress within 30 to 45 days of the original meeting. In working with different groups on various action plans, I have found that this is the maximum length of time to wait before holding a follow-up conversation. Any longer than this allows people to forget their accomplishments and to be more focused on reasons that some action was difficult to complete.

This progress review should include *both* what has been done as well as what has not been done. Try to resist a tendency to focus only on the problem areas. You should build the group's learning about its efforts from a balanced review of their experience so far.

Related Tools and Information

Using the tool I call **Three Follow-Up Questions** is a great way to structure an effective follow-up conversation.

Forces Review

Talking Constructively about Both Sides of an Idea

What Is It?

Forces Review is a process for leading a group through a balanced consideration of forces affecting achievement of some goal. It produces a range of ideas on possible actions for working with these forces.

Why Use It?

Discussions often focus on the difficulties restraining or threatening success on some goal. A more balanced consideration considers supporting as well as restraining forces affecting goal achievement. **Forces Review** provides for balanced review of all the forces, and then asks the group to identify how to strengthen supporting forces and limit the restraining forces.

How to Apply **Forces Review**

Clarify the goal under consideration and write this at the top of a flip chart. Explain that you want to complete a **Forces Review** to clarify how to move forward successfully.

Preparation:

- Write the goal at the top of a flip chart page.
- Draw a vertical line down the page under the goal to divide the page in half.

- On the left side of the divided page write "Supporting Forces" and draw an arrow pointing to the right. On the other side of the page write "Restraining Forces" and draw an arrow pointing to the left.

- Explain that the middle line is the current state. You are going to identify how various forces can shift the current state toward (to the right) or away from (to the left) achievement of the goal.

Try to focus only on the "Supporting Forces" first. These may be more difficult to identify.

Brainstorm. Begin with the "Supporting Forces" side. Ask the group to brainstorm the supporting forces that (will) help in fulfilling the goal. A supporting force could be almost anything, from people to resources to whatever seems likely to work in your favor. Conduct this as a true brainstorm: all ideas are valid and there should be no cross-questioning of different ideas. Write down suggestions as they arise under "Supporting Forces."

After the suggestions drop off, turn to "Restraining Forces" and repeat the brainstorm. This time write down the forces that are seen to hinder success.

Some item(s) may seem relevant to both lists, having both positive and negative impacts. If you have one of these, put it on both lists.

Multi-Voting. Once both lists are complete, give each participant six self-adhesive dots. Ask everyone to place dots on what s/he believes are the three most important items on the "Supporting Forces" list and on the three most important items under "Restraining Forces." Once all the dots have been placed, review the results and clarify what all have determined to be the top three forces in each category.

You may find it helpful to use more than one sheet of flip chart paper if your group is large or it's a complex goal. Rather than dividing one sheet of paper in half, place two sheets side by side, one labeled "Supporting Forces" and the other "Restraining Forces."

Possible actions. Focusing only on the top three "Supporting Forces," ask the group to identify ways to *strengthen* each of these factors. In what ways can the forces working towards the recommendation be made still more effective in helping to achieve success?

Then turn to the top three "Restraining Forces" and ask the group to identify specific ways to *weaken* each of these factors so that they are less of a barrier to success.

Conclusions. Finally, determine overall conclusions and next steps. What actions do the participants want to implement in light of this review?

Tip: What This Tool Is Not: This process is not a comparison of arguments for and against something, but rather an exploration of what may be working in favor of or contrary to the desired outcome. It should be an open recognition of different variables. If the discussion becomes more about why something should be done (or not), steer attention to the underlying forces that may be implied by some of the "should we/ shouldn't we" points.

Related Tools and Information

Future Focus and **Three Reaction Questions** are other tools for helping the group work with different views and opinions about some goal or decision. **Forces Review** is based on Force-Field Analysis as originally developed by Kurt Lewin. See the description of his work in Weisbord (2004, 82-83).

Four Responsibilities

Sharing the Work of Running the Meeting

What Is It?

Four Responsibilities describes necessary responsibilities that can be shared in conducting a more effective meeting.

Why Use It?

The responsibilities for an effective discussion are often overlooked or left to one person (e.g., meeting leader) to cover. This is a particular challenge when the leader is the person who has a lot to say on the subject. Giving different responsibilities to individual participants means that each responsibility can be better managed. Dividing up these responsibilities also creates a sense of shared ownership for meeting outcomes.

How to Apply **Four Responsibilities**

At the start of the meeting, ask for volunteers to share the following specific responsibilities:

Discussion Leader: Responsible for making sure each person who wants to speak is able to in the time available. This is not the presenter of some topic/proposal but someone who simply makes sure everyone gets to contribute.

Timekeeper: Keeps track of the time available. Alerts the group when time for a discussion is running out. When necessary, the timekeeper may raise a question about changing the agenda if it appears that more time may be needed for a particular discussion.

Recorder: Uses flip chart or white board to visibly record the progress of the group's discussion where all can see it. This should be done in a way that uses a few words to capture each speaker's comment(s).

Information manager/minutes: Responsible for maintaining the formal documentation and recorded minutes of the group's work.

Make sure each volunteer understands the scope of his/her responsibility for this meeting.

Caution on Recorder's Role: Some people will "record" by taking personal notes and transferring these to a flip chart at the end of discussion. This does not help the group keep track of its discussion and can take extra time when the recorder must then create the flip chart. Instead, encourage the recorder to write key phrases as they occur where all can see them. S/he doesn't have to be neat and spelling doesn't matter here.

Related Tools and Information

Supporting tools include **Visible Note Taking**. See Weisbord (2004, 439-440) for more on the evolution of small group facilitation.

Future Focus

Working on the Desired Future Rather Than Past Problems

What Is It?

Future Focus is a process for engaging participants in developing the desired future solution rather than focusing on solving past problems.

Why Use It?

Discussions about some necessary improvement or "fix" to a problem often get stuck in an analysis of what went wrong in the past. The discussion is difficult as people try to describe why something happened and who was responsible. This can create conflict and defensiveness, and limit development of better options.

When you focus the discussion on the future, you identify how things could be rather than how they were. This helps to maintain a more creative, energizing environment for discussion.

How to Apply **Future Focus**

There are two approaches:

The first approach is to frame the discussion by asking:

> *"How could this situation be handled better in the future?"*

Keep the focus on how it will be rather than an analysis of what went wrong. While you want to learn from past experience, the real opportunity is to describe what is desired and possible in the future.

In the second approach you begin by recalling and appreciating how things were in the past *when they were at their best*. That is, begin the discussion by recalling what participants know can be achieved because they have done it before. Ask participants to form pairs and interview each other as follows:

> "*Think of a time when we handled this very well. You felt pride in how this was managed. Tell the story of this time:*
>
> *1. What happened?*
>
> *2. Who was involved?*
>
> *3. What were you proud of achieving and how did this make you feel at the time?*"

Finally, ask the group to share what stands out from the stories of past success. Ask:

> "*How can this performance be true again in the future?*"

Related Tools and Information

The second approach is a version of **Positive Story Sharing. Forces Review** and **Three Reaction Questions** are other ways to build a balanced, open discussion of a difficult subject.

Ronald Lippitt was the first to note the value of a future focus in maintaining a more creative, positive group discussion. See Weisbord and Janoff (2010, 58-59) for more on his work. Aspects of the second approach are based in the principles of "appreciative inquiry." See Mohr and Watkins (2001) for an explanation of appreciative inquiry.

Go-Around

Hearing from Everyone Present

What Is It?

Go-Around involves giving each person a brief turn to speak to the topic, without interruption or comments. Everyone else listens. A **Go-Around** can be held at various points in the meeting from when people first gather to when you feel the discussion is ending, and the group is ready to reach a decision.

Why Use It?

It is important to give all participants a chance to speak and be heard. Some people will talk more than others. Some may remain silent. People may be making assumptions about the views of others. A **Go-Around** addresses these challenges and keeps all engaged.

At the beginning of a meeting, a **Go-Around** serves as an initial check-in. It provides an important opportunity for all participants to speak to the group briefly, making it more likely that they will continue to contribute.

A **Go-Around** is also helpful when the group seems to be getting stuck on some point. Complete a quick **Go-Around** asking for reflections on what participants now understand, or don't, regarding the original purpose of the discussion.

And a **Go-Around** is very useful when you want to reach a decision by consensus or consent with your group. (See **Five Cs**.)

How to Apply **Go-Around**

Ask participants to take turns offering a brief comment. Give a specific expectation for the time that each person has to speak—usually one to two minutes is enough. Explain that no one should speak twice before everyone has spoken once. This is an opportunity for everyone to hear from everyone else and not the time for any back-and-forth exchange of views.

Provide directions on what you want shared. At the start, as people first gather, this could be to share what each person needs to acknowledge is on his/her mind so s/he can be fully present. Or, it could be to share an expectation or wish for the outcome of the meeting. When used to build a decision, you can ask each person to describe his/her support or support with reservations.

You can proceed in order around the group, or you can allow people to speak in any order as long as all get to speak before anyone speaks twice.

Related Tools and Information

This tool was described in Weisbord and Janoff (2007, 55-56). Buck and Villines (2007) also provide a good explanation of this tool.

Go-Around^{VM}

Bringing Everyone into a Virtual Discussion

What Is It?

Go-Around^{VM} gives each person a brief turn to speak to the topic, without interruption. Everyone else listens. For a virtual meeting, you can conduct a **Go-Around^{VM}** at several points throughout a discussion. This is to ensure that anyone who might want to make a comment has an opportunity to do so.

Why Use It?

It is important to give all participants a chance to speak and be heard. Some people will talk more than others. Some may remain silent. People may be making assumptions about the views of others whether they hear from them or not. In a virtual meeting, it is particularly difficult to keep all included and know what each person is thinking. A **Go-Around^{VM}** addresses these challenges and keeps all engaged.

At the beginning of a virtual meeting, a **Go-Around^{VM}** serves as an initial check-in. It lets all know who is present and provides an opportunity for each participant to speak to the group. This makes it more likely s/he will continue to contribute to the meeting. A **Go-Around^{VM}** is also a great way to balance the contributions across participants meeting face-to-face and those participating from remote locations.

A **Go-Around^{VM}** is helpful when the group seems to be getting stuck on some point. Complete a quick **Go-Around^{VM}** asking for reflections on what participants now understand, or don't, regarding the original purpose of the discussion. And a **Go-Around**[VM] is very helpful when reaching decisions by consensus or consent (see **Five Cs**).

How to Apply **Go-Around**[VM]

When you begin a **Go-Around**[VM]:

- Set a specific expectation for how long each person should talk: usually a minute or so is enough.

- Explain that no one should speak twice before everyone has spoken once. It is not the time for any back-and-forth exchange of views and questions.

- Ask people to state their name when they start so all know who is speaking.

- Be clear about what you want shared: As you begin, the sharing could be what each person needs to acknowledge is on his/her mind so this can be set aside to be fully present. Or, it could be to share a wish for the outcome of the meeting. Later in the meeting, when building a decision, you can ask each person to describe his/her support or explain his/her support and any reservations.

Tip: It helps to have a picture of meeting participants in front of you as a reminder of who is speaking—or to whom they may wish to direct a question or comment.

Related Tools and Information

See Nancy Settle-Murphy (2012, 153-199) for more information on designing and conducting effective virtual meetings.

Hybrid Meeting Checklist[VM]

Working with Remote and Local Participants

What Is It?

The **Hybrid Meeting Checklist**[VM] is a set of guidelines for conducting effective discussions when some participants are meeting face-to-face while one or more others are "virtual participants" using audio conferencing or other technology.

Why Use it?

A mix of face-to-face and virtual participants usually puts the virtual participants at a significant disadvantage. Remote participants are less able to hear and see everything that goes on in the face-to-face setting, particularly any nonverbal communication. It also may be difficult for them to contribute to the discussion. However, there are various steps you can take to create more balanced participation.

How to Apply **Hybrid Meeting Checklist**[VM]

Plan and conduct your hybrid meeting using the suggestions below.

☐ Be sure the virtual participants can hear what is going on in the room. Use a good speakerphone in a central location. Keep any distracting noises—like paper shuffling—to a minimum.

☐ Bring the virtual participants into the face-to-face meeting by posting their pictures, or placing name tents on the table to "hold" a seat for them.

☐ Conduct frequent **Go-Arounds**[VM].

☐ Explain any nonverbal actions in the face-to-face meeting (for those who can't see what is going on in the room). This could include that someone is writing on a flip or that others are nodding, etc.

☐ Avoid doing anything in the meeting that puts virtual participants at a disadvantage because they can't see what is happening. Use **Visible Note Taking**[VM] with notes that can be shared on-line with virtual participants rather than a flip chart.

☐ Limit the time that remote participants are expected to attend the meeting. Have them participate for that part of the meeting where their input is needed, and don't expect them to stay connected for hours at a time.

☐ Ask each person present, virtual or face-to-face, to give their name when starting to speak.

☐ Do not allow side conversations in the meeting room since this is discourteous to the virtual participants.

Last, but not least, you can ask those participants who could be at the same location to stay in their offices and participate virtually instead—thereby avoiding the challenges of a hybrid meeting.

Related Tools and Information

See Nancy Settle-Murphy (2012, 170-172) for more on managing hybrid meetings. Also see related tools: **Meeting "Room" Checklist**[VM] and **Go-Around**[VM].

Meeting Room Checklist

Providing an Effective Physical Setting

What Is It?

This **Meeting Room Checklist** provides a set of requirements for a healthy meeting space, one that is more likely to support good, engaged conversation. Use this checklist to review your meeting space. Choose another space if your meeting room fails to meet these criteria, or look for ways to fix any deficiencies in the room you are using.

Why Use It?

Physical surroundings have a very real impact on the energy and focus of a meeting group. A meeting held under healthy physical conditions will improve the energy, creativity, and cooperation of everyone present.

How to Apply **Meeting Room Checklist**

Select a room and set up your space using this checklist:

☐ **Windows.** Daylight improves group energy, which is particularly important for longer meetings.

☐ **Sufficient space for people to hold subgroup meetings.** If the main meeting room is large enough, you can hold the subgroup meetings right in that room. Keeping the whole group together maintains the group's energy and avoids losing participants to other distractions. Use separate, break-out rooms only if your main room is too small to allow several groups to work in parallel without disturbing each other.

☐ **Walls for posting** group work (see **Visible Note Taking**).

☐ **Round tables.** If round tables are not available or if space is limited, use circles of chairs without tables.

☐ **No podiums** or other unnecessary furniture. Avoid a head table if possible.

☐ **Wireless microphones.** If microphones are necessary, make sure they can be moved around easily to where the participants are seated, rather than making the participants go to the microphone. Having participants go to a microphone will affect who chooses to speak and what gets said.

Related Tools and Information

Related tools include **Circle Up**, **Seating Structures**, and **Visible Note Taking**.

For more information see Weisbord and Janoff (2010, 221-225).

Meeting "Room" Checklist^VM

Providing an Effective Setting for Virtual Meetings

Meeting "Room" Checklist^VM

What Is It?

This **Meeting "Room" Checklist^VM** provides a set of requirements for an effective virtual meeting environment, one that is more likely to support and maintain participant engagement.

This checklist applies no matter what kind of technology you use. While a live video of all participants can make your meeting feel almost like you are in one room, you may be limited to using audio only and some way to share documents.

Why Use It?

The physical environment affects every meeting, face-to-face or virtual. The physical setting of virtual meetings may create conditions that "permit" a level of inattention and parallel processing that would be less likely in a face-to-face setting. However, a virtual meeting held under effective physical conditions will support better focus, more engagement, and productive use of time by all present.

How to Apply **Meeting "Room" Checklist**[VM]

Prepare for your virtual meeting using this checklist:

☐ **Participant location.** Your best choice is usually to have everyone take part in a virtual meeting rather than create a "hybrid" meeting with a mix of face-to-face and remote participants. A hybrid meeting puts those who are remote at a disadvantage to those meeting together. If some participants are in the same location, consider having them stay in their offices and sign in as if they were elsewhere. If you will have some participants seated together, then plan to facilitate the discussion in a way that balances remote and "local" input. See **Hybrid Meeting Checklist**.

☐ **Virtual meeting technology.** A means of providing visual support for the meeting is helpful. Use it if you can, but make sure it is accessible to everyone. Also make sure you know how to use it in advance of the meeting and check with participants to make sure they can use it too. Schedule and conduct a brief technology orientation session in advance of your meeting to help all get familiar with its use. Have someone available during the meeting who can handle technical problems should they arise.

☐ **Audio.**

- Avoid using speakerphones. Speakerphones (or audio through a computer) can result in background noise and audio interruptions. Some speakerphones also make it hard for others to contribute to the meeting, as the phone "cuts out" interjections. Instead, ask participants to use headsets and have them call into a common conference line or bridge number. This is much more effective than relying on the computer audio of any technology platform you are using.

- Ask participants not to use the mute button. Being on mute can cut out the background noise but enables more parallel processing and lower overall attention to the substance of the meeting. Use it only if there is excessive background noise.

- Encourage people to avoid using the "hold" button if they need to step away—a "hold" sometimes comes with distracting background music.

☐ **Pictures of participants.** It is always helpful to put a face together with a name and a voice. This is particularly important when people don't know each other well, but it is helpful in almost any virtual meeting. Some technology platforms show pictures of participants. If you don't have this capability, have participants provide a small self-portrait so you can put these together in advance and send them to everyone. Ask participants to keep the pictures in front of them as the meeting proceeds. As the leader, you can also use these pictures to keep track of who is contributing and whom to call on.

☐ **Visible notes in real time.** One of the best ways to keep a discussion focused and efficient is to make sure all can see the progress of the discussion through real-time notes. Ask a volunteer to take the notes as you lead a discussion (for more on this see **Visible Note Taking**^{VM}). Technology like Google Drive enables you to share a virtual "flip chart" so you can keep notes just as you would in a meeting room. Various technology platforms also let you to share a document so that anyone can add his/her comments as the discussion proceeds. Another option could be to use Skype, pointing the camera at the flip chart used for note taking.

☐ **Participant questions and interjections.** You want to make sure that participants can contribute to the discussion without interrupting others. This can be difficult since you can't see body language as you would in a face-to-face meeting. Some technologies support "virtual" hand raising and instant messaging, which can help if used appropriately. A simpler means of ensuring all get to speak is to stop every 10 minutes or so to check in with everyone on the subject of discussion. Do this by conducting a quick **Go-Around**^{VM} so each person can speak briefly to the point of the discussion.

Related Tools and Information

Related tools include **Hybrid Meeting Checklist**^{VM}, **Go-Around**^{VM}, and **Visible Note Taking**^{VM}. See Nancy Settle-Murphy (2012, 153-199) for more information on designing and conducting effective virtual meetings.

Multi-Voting

Showing Patterns of Preference

What Is It?

Multi-Voting helps participants explore their preferences on elements of some decision. This is usually done by placing colored, self-adhesive dots. Once the dots are placed, the whole group reviews the results and draws conclusions.

Why Use It?

Group discussion often leads to multiple options. This may reflect good, creative thinking from the group, but can make it hard to reach closure. **Multi-Voting** is designed to give the group information on how they individually and collectively view a range of issues, options, or ideas.

How to Apply **Multi-Voting**

There are two basic applications of this technique: priority setting and exploring positive/negative judgments. Below are the steps to follow for each application.

The steps for showing priority are:

1) Write the options or discussion points for review on a large piece of paper posted on a flip chart or the wall, where the whole group can gather to place their dots and review the results.

2) To show priority, give strips of self-adhesive colored dots (all in one color) to each participant. Use five to seven dots per person, depending on the number of individual items being prioritized.

- Strips of dots work better than asking people to make check marks, since each person knows how many dots s/he has to "spend" on choices. Using more than three dots means people do not have to think in terms of first, second, or third choices.

- You can use different colored dots for different participants if you think their views may vary by perspective and you want to see the pattern.

3) Explain that each person should put a dot on each item s/he views as most important relative to the task or decision. Participants should use all their dots and spread them around (or not) as they choose. They can even put them all on one item.

4) After all have placed their dots, ask the whole group to interpret the results. Raise questions like:

"Which items received the most dots?" "Which the least?"

"What surprises you about how the dots are distributed?"

"What relationships do you see across items that got many (or few) dots?"

The process for exploring *positive/negative* judgments is:

1) When you are evaluating a group of ideas or options, give participants strips of red and green dots. Provide as many red and as many green dots as there are options under consideration.

2) Ask everyone to place *either* a red *or* a green dot *on each* proposal/option. Explain that:

"Green means it is a good idea and has your support. Red means you have reservations or objections. You must place one dot (either red or green) on each idea."

3) After everyone has placed their dots, the whole group reviews the results:

"Which items received just green dots? We appear to be in agreement on these areas."

If there are many red dots on an option, ask:

Note: You do not have to ask who placed a particular red dot, only who wants to speak to the concern.

"Now looking at those items with quite a few red dots, can we just set these aside as unworkable for now?"

For those options receiving quite a few green dots, but one or a few red dot(s), ask:

"Who wants to speak to the red dot(s) on this item?"

Ask:

"Are there ways to address the concerns behind the red dot(s) to turn them to green, or do we set this aside as not agreed?"

Finally, you may propose to move forward with those options that are solid "green" while other items are held for reconsideration.

Related Tools and Information

Affinity Grouping may be used before **Multi-Voting** when there are many individual items to organize. **Multi-Voting** is particularly helpful for supporting consent or consensus decisions (see **Five Cs**), possibly with the help of the **80/20 Principle**.

PALPaR

Creating a Respectful Exchange in Response to Some Proposal

What Is it?

PALPaR is a process for gathering feedback on some proposal or plan in a way that supports reflection and listening to any comments before responding. The acronym summarizes the process:

- **P**resent
- **A**sk
- **L**isten
- **P**ause, **a**nd
- **R**eply

Why Use It?

An awkward situation can arise after a plan or proposal is presented. Some participants share quick judgments while others are quiet. Questions may have to be addressed in the moment with little chance for reflection. What participants like about the proposal may get overlooked. It can be difficult to have a thoughtful, respectful exchange of ideas.

PALPaR enables participants to develop and share their reactions. They then see that their comments have been heard. It creates an opportunity for you (or the person making the proposal) to give a thoughtful response without having to reply quickly or off-the-cuff.

How to Apply **PALPaR**

Before presenting a plan or proposal, outline the following steps to participants, and then apply the process as described.

Present: You (or someone else) present(s) the proposal (report or other information).

Ask: Then you ask participants to talk with each other (in small groups) to answer three "reaction" questions, such as:

- *"What did you like about this proposal?"*
- *"Where do you need more information?"*
- *"Where do you have concerns?"*

Listen: Take reports from each small group, one question at a time. That is, take everyone's comments on the first question about "likes" first, before going to the second question. As you hear the replies, record key points where all can see. (See **Visible Note Taking** tool.)

Pause: Then take a specified break to incorporate what you have heard before continuing. This may range from a 15-minute coffee break, to an overnight break, or a break until the next meeting. Use this pause to reflect on feedback received and decide how to respond. You do not have to change your proposal in response to the feedback, but you do need to give the feedback consideration and show you heard it.

Reply: Come back to the group and summarize what you heard as key points in the feedback. Then explain how you have taken that feedback into account (or not) in the final proposal and provide additional information as relevant.

Related Tools and Information

PALPaR works well with **1-2-All** in supporting a structure of small group discussion before reporting out. However, **PALPaR** is specifically used in response to some proposal or presentation and can be used with different-sized groups. It's best used with the "consult" approach to decisions (see **Five Cs**). Other supporting tools include **Visible Note Taking** and **Three Reaction Questions**.

PALPaR is based on a process developed by Kathleen Dannemiller and colleagues. See Dannemiller Tyson Associates (2000) and Jacobs (1994) for more about their designs.

Positive Story Sharing

Building Understanding of Common Experiences

What Is It?

Positive Story Sharing (PSS) gives everyone a chance to share examples from his/her experience. This tool is best used near the beginning of a meeting, particularly when participants may not know each other well. Much like **1-2-All**, it enables individuals to reflect and share their thoughts in small groups, but here the focus is on sharing stories of positive personal experiences in some aspect of the work of this meeting.

Why Use it?

Positive Story Sharing helps create conditions for more productive conversations because it helps us connect with each other around what is positive and energizing. Use **PSS** at the beginning of a meeting when you need more open sharing. This is particularly true when some participants do not know others, or there are differences in status or hierarchy. **PSS** is also useful as a team reviews its past work, enabling it to recognize progress rather than focus only on remaining tasks and difficulties.

How to Apply **Positive Story Sharing**

Clarify the focus for stories to be shared and proceed as follows:

Individual Reflection. Check to make sure everyone under-stands the request to recall a specific successful incident relative to the purpose of the discussion. Give everyone a minute or two to gather his/her thoughts.

Small Group Discussion. Next ask participants to form small, two to three person groups. Explain that each person will be both an interviewer and an interviewee. The interviewer helps the interviewee share his/her story in detail. The interviewer follows the outline below. You can place this outline on a flip chart for everyone to see.

- *"Tell me about a time when you felt very good about your success with (discussion purpose)."*
- *"What happened? Who was involved?"*
- *"What made this so successful?"*

Define the time available and ask them to make sure all in their group are interviewed in that period.

Whole Group Report. Have each person share his/her story with the whole group (with the help of their interviewer.) You can also choose to sample stories, one per small group, if hearing every story would take too long.

Conclusion. After sharing stories, discuss the following with everyone:

- *"What are we learning about our experiences with …?"*
- *"What should we remember to make these positive expe-riences happen more of the time?"*

Related Tools and Information

PSS is derived from Appreciative Inquiry (Whitney and Tro-sten-Bloom, 2003, Ludema et al., 2003). As a tool to build the conditions for productive conversations, it can fulfill some of the conditions identified by researcher Solomon Asch as further defined by Trist and Emery (Weisbord et al., 1992, ch. 2). The process outlined above is a version of **1-2-All**.

Presentations In Perspective (PIP)

Ensuring that Presentations Support Discussion

What Is It?

PIP (Presentations In Perspective) is a set of guidelines for placing presentations in the context of the work of a meeting so they support effective discussion.

Why Use It?

A presentation can have both intended and unintended impacts on how participants engage in the work of the meeting. It can provide necessary context and background for the discussion. It also can be an informative update on key goals or provide expert information the group needs. However, a presentation that goes on too long or is poorly delivered can make listeners think that their contributions are not important. Or that communication in this meeting will be mostly one-way and that maybe now is a good time to check email.

Note: The focus of this book is on tools for meetings where you want an exchange of ideas among participants. See other sources for communication guidelines on making effective presentations.

How to Apply **PIP**

Keep presentations short. They should be no more than 15 minutes. After 15 minutes, attention is likely to drop and participants become used to taking a passive role in the meeting. If the presentation needs to be longer, break it up into separate sections with opportunities for group interaction in between.

Use presentations only to provide the overall framework of the subject. Provide handouts or exhibits with additional detail for participants to review on their own. This makes it less likely that presentations will cover too much content, and respects participants' ability to review the materials on their own.

Try not to begin the meeting with a presentation. Engage participants first. People are more likely to contribute after a presentation if they have already had a chance to speak in the meeting.

Make sure that the presentation serves the work of the meeting. It should be clear exactly how or why this information will help the group's discussion. Avoid the use of presentations as simply a sign of respect for some figure of authority who wants to address the group.

Set specific expectations for participants. Set clear expectations for the presentation's purpose by telling participants what they should listen for and be prepared to discuss afterwards.

Related Tools and Information

PALPaR provides a helpful overall process for the place of a presentation in the group's work.

Seating Arrangements

Changing Interaction by Changing Seating

What Is It?

Seating Arrangements is a reminder to consider how participants, including the leader, are seated. How you are seated can have an impact on dialogue and decision making.

Why Use It?

You can create better, more balanced participation by giving all a "good" seat at the table no matter their status. You should avoid the impression that one area is where the power and influence reside.

It is important to consider how you want people seated if you are inviting new or different participants. But it is particularly important if you plan to use small group discussion (e.g., **1-2-All**). In such situations, thinking about seating in advance can improve your discussion.

How to Apply **Seating Arrangements**

Decide whether you want particular individuals to sit together: Is there a reason for some people to sit with each other or not? Most of the time the best choice is to mix participants so that the same people don't sit with and talk to the same folks as usual.

Plan to direct people to their assigned seats as *they arrive*. You don't want to move people around once they sit down. Some will resist changing seats.

- If there are materials for the meeting, you can put participant names on the packets and place them in front of chairs in the desired locations.

- At the very least, you can just take a different chair yourself. If you always sit at the head of the table, move to the side and see how others adjust their seats.

- If it's a large group, create small circles of chairs.

- Whatever approach you use, it helps to explain why you are changing the seating. You can point out that you want to create the opportunity for new and different exchanges.

Related Tools and Information

Related tools include **Circle Up** and **Meeting Room Checklist**.

Where people sit has a powerful influence on dynamics of everyday meetings. For example, see McConnon, "You Are Where You Sit: How to Decode the Psychology of the Morning Meeting." *Business Week*, July 23, 2007, 66-67.

STARS

Creating One Plan to Manage All

What Is It?

STARS is an acronym that stands for the five guidelines for an effective meeting agenda. Such an agenda lays out the design for the whole meeting and may contain more than one task to be completed.

Why Use It?

Participants can help the leader stay on time and on track when they all have a clear understanding of the work to be done. Providing a well-defined agenda (using the **STARS** guidelines) and sharing it ahead of time gives all a chance to prepare and to participate effectively.

Some leaders prefer sharing a fairly general agenda with participants. They want to have more flexibility in reallocating the time or sequence of meeting activities. However, this leaves all the responsibility for facilitating the meeting with the leader. As a result, participants are less likely to share responsibility for meeting success, and timing or meeting outcomes may suffer.

How to Apply **STARS**

Use these five guidelines in creating an agenda:

Specific: Points to be covered are explicitly defined in terms of their purpose or intended outcome. (For more, see the **FATT** tool for defining the purpose.)

Timed and sequenced: Each part of the agenda has an assigned period of time. The **FATT** definition of various tasks includes specific timing, but there are often check-ins, updates on past actions, and other meeting activities that need time as well.

The sequence of activities should be considered. The most important pieces of meeting work should come near the beginning of the meeting to make sure that they aren't arbitrarily shortened for lack of time.

Actionable: Each task of the meeting should lead to some action as a result of discussion. That is, there should be value in the two-way exchange of information, or else why meet? For example, if this meeting is held as a monthly update, ask what actions will participants take as a result of the update? If this is not clear, consider sharing information in ways other than a face-to-face meeting.

Relevant: The work of the meeting should be relevant to those attending the meeting. If some points are not relevant to everyone, then the meeting should be designed to allow people to attend the part of the meeting that is most relevant for them.

Shared: Meeting participants should have a copy of the agenda well in advance so they can be prepared.

Many Short Items?

Be wary of an agenda that has many five-minute items. If these are "updates," maybe they could be handled in a memo. If they need to receive a vote for the record, but don't need real discussion, put them together as a "consent item" that the group can vote on accepting as a group. If real discussion is needed around some of these points, consider grouping them under one overall point on the agenda, defining the intended outcome, and providing an appropriate amount of time for discussion.

Related Tools and Information

Related or supporting tools include **FATT** for defining the task, **Time Planning Tips** for planning the overall use of time, **PIP** for planning the place of presentations, and other tools as necessary to support the various choices for planning your meeting.

Three Follow-Up Questions

Learning from a Balanced Review of Progress

What Is It?

Three Follow-Up Questions consists of three questions that should be asked in any follow-up discussion. These questions set up a productive review of progress building upon what can be learned from all efforts so far, successful or not.

Why Use It?

A follow-up conversation can be a difficult, ineffective discussion. Some participants may be focused on explaining what made it difficult to complete planned actions. Meanwhile, actual accomplishments receive less attention or are overlooked.

How to Apply Three Follow-Up Questions

Bring the group together and focus the discussion around these three questions:

1. *"What has been accomplished as planned?"*

2. *"What hasn't been accomplished as planned?"*

3. *"What can we learn about making progress in this area from our answers to questions 1 and 2?"*

Use all the questions in this order. Balance time and attention across all three questions. You can modify the questions to fit the circumstances, but keep all three types.

Related Tools and Information

See **Follow-Up Timing** for guidance on when to hold a follow-up conversation.

Three Reaction Questions

Gathering Balanced Feedback

What Is It?

Three Reaction Questions supports balanced feedback on a proposal, idea, or decision. It begins with individual reflection on three questions before sharing responses to those questions, one at a time, beginning with a question about what people like before going on to concerns.

Why Use It?

You can face several challenges to balanced feedback when a proposal is presented in a meeting. Those challenges include:

- Hearing first from those who "think on their feet" and react right away.

- Hearing first (or only) about the various concerns and not about what people like about the proposal.

- Hearing only from a few individuals who seem to dominate the discussion.

By reflecting on their reactions before speaking, participants can consider the range of their thoughts. Participants then hear more balanced feedback as they all listen to each other's likes, as well as questions and concerns.

How to Apply Three Reaction Questions

After you present the proposal, ask participants to reflect on their own or (even better) to talk in small groups to answer the questions below. Try not to take any questions at first, as this will open up the discussion before you give them all a chance to reflect on their reactions.

1. "What do you like about [the proposal]?"

2. "Where do you need further information?"

3. "Where do you have concerns?"

After a few minutes, take reports (from individuals or small groups), one question at a time beginning with the first. Make sure you get all replies to the first question before proceeding to the second.

Once all the reactions have been shared, ask the group,

"What are we learning about this proposal/decision?"

This last question is intended to help everyone integrate all that s/he heard and arrive at overall conclusions.

Related Tools and Information

Go-Around and **1-2-All** are additional ways to support balanced discussion. **Three Reaction Questions** can help a group reach a decision using any of the **Five Cs**.

Three Reaction Questions is adapted from a process developed by Kathleen Dannemiller and colleagues (Dannemiller Tyson Associates, 2000, Jacobs, 1994).

Time Planning Tips

Planning and Managing
a Scarce Resource

What Is It?

Time Planning Tips is a collection of practices for productive use of time in meetings.

Why Use It?

Time in meetings should be planned and spent as if it were money—which in a way it is. Meetings take people away from other responsibilities, and it is a true loss if time is not well spent. Unfortunately, most meetings use time inefficiently, frustrating participants as well as leaders. This tool can help you spend meeting time efficiently and effectively.

How to Apply **Time Planning Tips**

Use the following tips and recommendations to plan how you want to engage participants in discussions and decisions on a task-by-task basis.

Clearly specify (in writing) the work to be done. Many meetings waste time because participants don't all have the same understanding of what it is they are trying to accomplish. A clear statement of the meeting task can help (see **FATT**). Also, each time you request participants to work on something in small groups, you should provide clear directions along with a specific amount of time to complete the work. These instructions should be written, not verbal, for ongoing reference.

Plan for individual reflection and small group sharing. A tool like **1-2-All** enables everyone to collect his/her thoughts and have a chance to speak to the topic. It is also a great way to manage time so that everyone is able to speak and the total time for conversation is fixed.

Use multiple, concurrent small groups to hold parallel discussions. Small group conversations (e.g., **1-2-All**) enable a point that could require considerable time for the whole group to discuss to be fully considered in less time. Everyone gets to share his/her thoughts, at least in a small group. You can also give different assignments to different small groups so that more aspects of a subject can be considered at one time.

Plan agenda timing realistically. Try not to have an agenda with many short items that are each supposed to take a few minutes to cover. The difficulty with multiple short items is that they give a false sense of what can be accomplished in the meeting. The more short topics on an agenda, the greater the likelihood that time will slip by a few minutes on each item and eventually throw the whole agenda off schedule.

- If group comment or input is expected, there is little likelihood that an item will take only a few minutes. Allow at least 10 minutes for any point requiring discussion.

- Consider whether any short "updates" might be better communicated in a memo outside of the meeting.

Limit presentations to 15 minutes or less. Try to limit formal presentations to 15 minutes or less (20 minutes at the outside). Shorter presentations are more likely to communicate key points more effectively. If the presentation really needs to be longer, break it up into separate sections with opportunities for group interaction in between. Long presentations send an unspoken message that participants are here to listen, not contribute. The level of interaction will go down. See **PIP** for more.

Allow participants to co-manage the work to the time available. Share responsibility for managing time with participants. Plan and communicate the intended time available for all aspects of the agenda. Ask someone to be the timekeeper and stress that s/he should let the group know when there are two minutes left on a given item. With a two-minute warning, the group can wrap up the discussion, or you can ask them if they want to change the agenda to add more time. (See **Four Responsi-bilities** for more on timekeeping.)

Control time for group reports to whole group. When you have multiple small groups that need to report back to the whole group, the reports can be redundant and lengthy. You can avoid these problems by one of these means:

- "Popcorn" reports: Take a sample of the various small group conclusions by calling on a few groups to share theirs, and then checking with others as to whether they had further/ different points to share.

- Give each group a strict time limit for reporting, and ask the timekeeper to help you manage reports to the time available. Most small group reports can be kept to three to five minutes or less if that is specified in advance.

When groups are working on more than one question, take replies to one question at a time. Ask for one group to report their answer to the first question, then ask the other groups for *additions just on that first question.* Then go to another group and ask them to report on the second question and repeat the process. This avoids redundant reporting and keeps the process moving and building.

Related Tools and Information

Related or supporting tools include **1-2-All** and **Go-Around**, as they help you to set up efficient participation or to subdivide the work. **PIP (Presentations In Perspective)** and **Four Responsibilities** help you manage other aspects of timing. The results of your planning should be part of a **STARS** agenda.

Time Planning Tips^{VM}

Planning and Managing a Scarce Resource in Virtual Meetings

Time Planning Tips^{VM}

What Is It?

Time Planning Tips^{VM} provides recommendations for structuring a productive use of time in a virtual meeting.

Why Use It?

Time in meetings is always precious. Virtual meetings are no exception. Furthermore, virtual meetings need to be kept relatively short (60 to 90 minutes) to keep people engaged. In addition, they almost always need to end on time with no opportunity for running over.

How to Apply **Time Planning Tips^{VM}**

Plan and conduct your virtual meeting using the following tips:

Create a detailed STARS agenda to help you and participants manage time and activities on the call. The design of this agenda is basically the same as for a face-to-face meeting. However, for virtual meetings make sure to consider the following:

- Plan time for a **Go-Around^{VM}** as you start. As the meeting begins, it is important to conduct a quick check-in, so all get a chance to speak and everyone knows who is here. This can also help you start on time even if some participants arrive late.

- Assign a realistic amount of time for discussions on agenda items. Plan time for engaging participants in the discussion through a **Go-Around** or possibly a poll.

- Schedule most important, and presumably longer, items early in the meeting so that they aren't the ones to be cut if you run out of time.

Limit presentations to 15 minutes *or less* for virtual meetings. Long presentations make it more likely that participants will disengage and direct their attention elsewhere. Avoid this by sending out materials in advance. During the meeting you can summarize what was sent in a couple of points on a slide and then move to discussion. See **PIP** for more.

Clearly specify the work and agenda for the meeting. Virtual meeting participants need a clear understanding of the work of the meeting, and this should be sent out in advance. At the start of the virtual session, briefly review the agenda to orient everyone to how they will spend time on this call.

Start the meeting on time with all technology ready to go. Nothing threatens the use of time right from the beginning quite like participants' having problems signing in. To avoid this, encourage everyone to sign in early to make sure all is working. You may also want to provide some one-on-one support in advance of the meeting for those participants using the technology for the first time.

Minimize the disruption of late arrivals. Once the meeting begins, minimize the interruptions from any late arrivals. Virtual meeting leaders tend to stop a discussion and recap its progress each time someone joins. This wastes everyone's time. Instead, acknowledge the addition of a new participant so all know who is present, and remind everyone of where the group is in the discussion. Then just keep going. If everyone has a clear agenda, anyone joining late should understand the progress of the meeting to this point.

Related Tools and Information

Related or supporting tools include **Go-Around**[VM] to build efficient participation, **PIP (Presentations In Perspective)**, and **Five Responsibilities**[VM]. The results of your planning should help you create a realistic **STARS** agenda. See Nancy Settle-Murphy for more on virtual meeting agendas (2012, 154-158).

Time Renegotiation

Keeping Everyone Responsible for Managing Time

What Is It?

Time Renegotiation is a practice of openly involving participants in the reallocation of available time when meeting demands change the original plan.

Why Use It?

When the task and timing are clear, it is possible to renegotiate the necessary time with participants as circumstances require. In this way, the whole group shares responsibility for managing how time is spent.

How to Apply **Time Renegotiation**

If you are running longer than planned, stop the discussion and ask the group what they would like to do.

- Can time be taken from some later item on the agenda and used here?

- Is the group willing to continue this discussion for (some stated amount of time), even if it means running over time for the meeting as a whole?

If the meeting is ahead of schedule, explicitly adjust the overall schedule for later points so that you save the time you've gained and don't run the meeting out to its original length by spending more time than necessary on later items.

Related Tools and Information

Supporting tools include **Time Planning Tips** and **Four Responsibilities**. Having a dedicated timekeeper is very helpful to this process—particularly if the timekeeper alerts the group to the remaining time for some discussion before time runs out. Overall time management is aided with a clear **STARS** agenda.

Visible Note Taking

Recording the Progress of the Group's Discussion

What Is It?

Visible Note Taking involves recording the progress of the group's discussions on a surface all can see. It also shows each participant that his or her comments were heard and recognized.

Why Use It?

Many meetings have minutes. While these provide a record, they don't aid the progress of discussion in the meeting. In a longer discussion, meeting participants can lose track of what has been said and how the group's comments are (hopefully) building toward conclusions. Writing out notes of key comments and decisions where all can see them keeps the discussion on track. These real-time notes can also support any minutes prepared after the meeting.

How to Apply **Visible Note Taking**

Maintain an ongoing record of comments, using each speaker's words as much as possible.

Record the comments where all can see them. Best choice is usually a flip chart. Some abbreviation of comments is fine as long as you capture the essence of what the speaker said.

You can use headlines, different colored pens, or other means to highlight and organize the information on the pages as you go.

Plan Where and How You Will Take Notes to Serve the Work

Arrange for a note-taking area in view of the whole group.

- A flip chart is often the best because you have multiple pages and the completed pages can be posted on a wall to keep them visible as you need more space. Avoid just turning over pages on a flip chart, since this hides previous notes from the group's sight. A white board or black board can work as well, but you have to manage the notes to the space available.

- If you expect to generate many ideas and want to use **Affinity Grouping** later as you build decisions, you can take notes on large sticky notes, one idea or comment per sticky note.

- If you take notes on a computer, have an LCD projector to show the screen of notes as they are entered. But a computer makes it difficult to use other tools like **Multi-Voting** and **Affinity Grouping**, so this is not always a good choice.

Related Tools and Information

Affinity Grouping is an aid in organizing many diverse contributions. **Four Responsibilities** reminds you to divide up roles and allows the recorder to fulfill just this one role.

Visible Note Taking^{VM}

Recording the Progress of the Virtual Meeting Discussion

What Is It?

Visible Note Taking^{VM} involves recording the progress of the group's discussions on a surface all can see. It also shows each participant that his or her comments were heard and recognized.

Why Use It?

In a virtual discussion, participants can lose track of what has been said and how the group's comments are (hopefully) building toward conclusions. Seeing an ongoing record of comments assures each person that his/her contributions have been recognized.

How to Apply **Visible Note Taking**^{VM}

Maintain an ongoing record of comments, using each speaker's words as much as possible. Abbreviations are fine; just get the essence of comments.

Plan where and how you will take notes. Use a form of technology that enables all participants to see the notes evolve as the discussion proceeds. In a hybrid meeting with some face-to-face participants, you will want to make sure that remote participants have the same information as the local, face-to-face participants, and vice versa. This means that face-to-face participants may have to be on their computers to see the notes as if they were remote, or you can project a computer screen in the meeting room as you make the notes.

- Use technology that is accessible to all. If you don't have the ability to share a screen or use an electronic whiteboard or other technology, you can still share a document on Google Drive on which you type the notes of the discussion as it proceeds.

- Test the use of the technology for note taking before the meeting so you know how it works and are sure that all can see it.

Related Tools and Information

Five Responsibilitiesᵛᴹ reminds you to divide up roles and allows the recorder to fulfill just this one role.

Endnotes

ⁱ Marvin Weisbord spoke to this point at a master class of facilitators in Philadelphia in September, 2014.

ⁱⁱ Brian used each tool in the course of the meeting without calling attention to the process he was using. As explained later in this book, it would not have been helpful to draw attention to the choice he made to employ some structure or process. He just applied it.

ⁱⁱⁱ **PALPaR** is based on a process originally defined by Kathleen Dannemiller (see Dannemiller Tyson Associates, 2000, or Jacobs, 1994.)

^{iv} **Three Reaction Questions** comes from the work of Kathleen Dannemiller (see Dannemiller Tyson Associates, 2000, or Jacobs, 1994.)

^v See James Surowiecki, *The Wisdom of Crowds* (Doubleday, 2004) for more. Jonah Lehrer writing in *The New Yorker* on "Group Think" (January 30, 2012, pp. 22-27) also highlights research on the importance of exchanging diverse views in creative thinking. *Scientific American* published an article by Katherine Phillips (Sept. 16, 2014) summarizing a variety of studies showing how being with a diverse group of people makes us more creative and dedicated to doing a good job at something. Finally, Cass Sunstein and Reid Hastie summarize much of the recent research and provide ideas for improving group decisions in *Wiser: Getting Beyond Groupthink to Make Groups Smarter* (Harvard Business Review Press, 2015).

^{vi} Based upon the research of Solomon Asch as adapted by Eric Trist and Fred Emery (Weisbord et al.,1992, ch. 2).

^{vii} A pattern of such a mismatch in decision-making expectations has been described at Chrysler and GM before they both went through bankruptcy. See Steven Rattner, *Overhaul* (2010, p.196) for a description of what was known as the "GM Nod."

^{viii} This is sometimes referred to as the common ground approach to consensus. It is based on the assumption that in any given situation, people meeting together will agree on 80% of some issue. It is the remaining 20% that causes them to get stuck and fail to reach consensus, or to "cave in" to group pressure. For more on consensus decision making, see Marvin Weisbord and Sandra Janoff, *Don't Just Do Something, Stand There!* (Berrett-Koehler, 2007, pp. 81-95) and Larry Dressler, *Consensus Through Conversation* (Berrett-Koehler, 2006).

^{ix} Consent decisions are well described in *We the People: Consenting to a Deeper Democracy* by John Buck and Sharon Villines (Sociocracy. Info, 2007).

^x The main work of this meeting was to consider the use of the "Transition Town" model for this committee's work with the community. This model is quite elaborate with many steps and details. The 12-member committee had previously seen a presentation on the model and the main work of this meeting would be deciding whether/how to use it.

^{xi} The original four roles included a "reporter" and no "information manager." I have revised that role here for more general meeting use apart

from the large group meetings that are the focus of Weisbord and Janoff's work.

[xii] Rob Kaufman was the facilitator of this committee and with committee chair Ellen Sturgis did a great job keeping it working productively.

[xiii] For more about the advantages of acknowledging but not "working" areas of disagreement see Weisbord and Janoff (2010, p. 87).

[xiv] I first heard these questions used by my colleague, Jim Van Patten.

[xv] I am not concerned here with the type of virtual meeting technology in use. Technology is changing and getting better all the time. All of the recommendations assume that there is at least a phone line for audio and some form of internet connection for sharing documents or screens. Such basic assumptions about technology mean these recommendations can apply to more sophisticated technology. Better technology just makes it easier to use the structural approaches recommended here.

[xvi] There are many ways to do this, including sharing a computer screen or using something like Google Drive.

[xvii] Robert Kaufman focused on facilitating the committee meetings. He found various ways to help the group build toward the decisions without splitting into factions. The committee chair was Ellen Sturgis, and she did an excellent job of steering the overall process.

[xviii] For more on the evolution of large group methods, see Bunker and Alban (1997), Weisbord et al. (1992), and Weisbord (2004, chapter 19).

[xix] I wasn't the only one working on application of large group practices to other meetings. As I was completing this book, Henri Lipmanowicz and Keith McCandless published *The Surprising Power of Liberating Structures* that contains many similar recommendations and ideas.

[xx] We weren't the only ones to observe this. Future Search has been used around the world in every setting and culture imaginable. This has also held true for other large group methods (e.g., Open Space and World Café.)

[xxi] Marie McCormick and Donna Skubis Pearce were important early thought partners with me on this journey.

References

Agazarian, Yvonne M. and Susan P. Gantt. *Autobiography of a Theory: Developing a Theory of Living Systems and Its Systems-Centered Practice.* London: Jessica Kingsley, 2000.

Axelrod, Dick and Emily Axelrod. *Let's Stop Meeting Like This.* San Francisco: Berrett-Koehler, 2014.

Baldwin, Christina, and Ann Linea. *The Circle Way—A Leader in Every Chair.* San Francisco: Berrett-Koehler, 2010.

Brown, Juanita, and David Isaacs. *The World Café: Shaping Our Futures Through Conversations That Matter.* San Francisco: Berrett-Koehler, 2005.

Buck, John and Sharon Villines. *We the People: Consenting to a Deeper Democracy.* Washington: Sociocracy.info, 2007.

Bunker, Barbara Benedict and Billie T. Alban. *The Handbook of Large Group Methods.* San Francisco: Jossey-Bass Wiley, 2006.

Bunker, Barbara Benedict and Billie T. Alban. *Large Group Interventions.* San Francisco: Jossey-Bass, 1997.

Dannemiller Tyson Associates. *Whole Scale Change: Unleashing the Magic in Organizations.* San Francisco: Berrett-Koehler, 2000.

Dixon, Nancy M. *Perspectives on Dialogue.* Greensboro, NC: Center for Creative Leadership, 1996.

Holman, Peggy, Tom Devane, and Steven Cady, eds. *The Change Handbook*, 2nd ed. San Francisco: Berrett-Koehler, 2007.

Jacobs, Robert W. *Real Time Strategic Change.* San Francisco: Berrett-Koehler, 1994.

Lehrer, Jonah. "Group Think." *The New Yorker*, January 30, 2012, pp. 22-27.

Lipmanowicz, Henri and Keith McCandless. *The Surprising Power of Liberating Structures: Simple Rules to Unleash a Culture of Innovation.* Seattle, WA: Liberating Structures Press, 2013.

Ludema, James, Diana Whitney, Bernard Mohr, Thomas Griffin. *The Appreciative Inquiry Summit.* San Francisco: Berrett-Koehler, 2003.

McConnon, Aili. "You Are Where You Sit: How to Decode the Psychology of the Morning Meeting." *Business Week*, July 23, 2007, pp.66-67.

Mohr, Bernard J. and Jane Magruder Watkins, *Appreciative Inquiry: Change at the Speed of Imagination.* San Francisco: Jossey-Bass Pfeiffer, 2001.

Owen, Harrison. *Open Space Technology: A User's Guide.* San Francisco: Berrett-Koehler, 1997.

Perkins, David. *King Arthur's Round Table: How Collaborative Conversations Create Smart Organizations.* Hoboken, NJ: Wiley, 2003.

Phillips, Katherine W. "How Diversity Makes Us Smarter." *Scientific American*, September 16, 2014.

Robert, H.M. III, Daniel H. Honemann, Thomas J. Balch, Daniel E. Seabold, Shmuel Gerber. *Robert's Rules of Order Newly Revised,* 11th ed. Cambridge, MA: Da Capo Press, 2011.

Settle-Murphy, Nancy. *Leading Effective Virtual Teams.* Boca Raton, FL, 2013.

Sunstein, Cass, and Reid Hastie. *Wiser: Getting Beyond Groupthink to Make Groups Smarter.* Cambridge, MA: Harvard Business Review Press, 2015.

Surowieki, James. *The Wisdom of Crowds.* New York: Doubleday, 2004.

Weisbord, Marvin R., and Sandra Janoff. *Don't Just Do Something, Stand There! Ten Principles for Leading Meetings That Matter.* San Francisco: Berrett-Koehler, 2007.

Weisbord, Marvin R., and Sandra Janoff. *Future Search: Getting the Whole System in the Room for Vision, Commitment, and Action.* San Francisco: Berrett-Koehler, 2010.

Weisbord, Marvin R. *Productive Workplaces Revisited.* San Francisco: Jossey-Bass, 2004.

Weisbord, Marvin R., et al. *Discovering Common Ground.* San Francisco: Berrett-Koehler, 1992.

Whitney, Diana, and Amanda Trosten-Bloom. *The Power of Appreciative Inquiry: A Practical Guide to Positive Change.* San Francisco: Berrett-Koehler, 2003.

Acknowledgments

The journey that led to this book began when I first met Marvin Weisbord and Sandra Janoff and saw them lead a large group discussion. Their approach to helping groups engage in dialogue and decision making is known as Future Search. Over the years I have learned much from them both. This book would not have been possible without their insights and support. In addition, I want to thank Nancy Settle-Murphy for her collaboration on approaches to structuring better virtual meetings.

A number of colleagues and clients have provided important support in the development of ideas for structuring better meetings. In particular I want to thank Breck Arnzen, Bruce Bacon, Joseph Carrabis, Nick Craig, Joe Durzo, John Eggert, John Haskell, Rob Kaufman, John Roberts, Ellen Sturgis, and Jim Van Patten. All of them have trusted me to design critical meetings for their organizations or have taken my suggestions to try on their own. They have also spent hours reviewing my drafts and helping me clarify key ideas. I have learned much from their support and feedback. Marie McCormick and Donna Skubis Pearce were early partners in this effort and I remain grateful to them as my "thought-partners" at the beginning of this journey.

Many authors thank their spouse and families for their support. In my case, I know this book simply would not have been possible without the personal and professional support of my wife, Sharon Brownfield. Sharon has served as my best coach and colleague all along the way. Thank you!

Finally, *Leading Great Meetings* would not be possible without the professional efforts of two friends: Susan Rardin for her editing, and Betsy Stepp for graphic design.

Index

Page references in **boldface** indicate the main explanation or description.

About the Author

Richard Lent has spent more than 25 years identifying structures for more effective meetings and coaching leaders in their use. He has facilitated meetings for strategic planning, organizational change and community issues. Rick has also helped nonprofit boards redefine strategy, resolve governance issues, and improve teamwork. Among his clients are the World Food Programme, USAID, UNICEF, the WK Kellogg Foundation, and the International Red Cross. He has also assisted various civic, religious and nonprofit groups of all sizes.

Prior to starting his own consulting business, Rick managed consulting and training organizations for Omega Performance Corporation, Digital Equipment Corporation and the University of Maryland. He received his Ph.D. from Syracuse University in Instructional Design, Development and Evaluation and continued his studies in organizational learning and development.

Leading Great Meetings is his second book. In 2012 he published the *Meeting for Results Tool Kit* that provided an abbreviated introduction to the tools and concepts of this new approach.

Rick shares ideas for better meetings on his blog at **www.meetingforresults.com/blog**.

You can reach him at **rick@meetingforresults.com**.

Visit **www.meetingforresults.com** for more information and help with your meetings. There you will find pdfs of the Meeting Culture Survey materials and also a guide to Meeting Evaluation that you can download. You can also find more stories and examples of structural approaches to challenging meetings on Rick's blog.

Want to introduce a better way of meeting to your organization? Rick offers custom webinars and workshops to help you adopt and adapt these recommendations to your meeting challenges. Contact him at **rick@meetingforresults.com** to learn more.

73236751R00127

Made in the USA
Lexington, KY
08 December 2017